A VERY SPECTRUM CHRISTMAS

Thomas A. Christie

Other Books by
Thomas A. Christie

Liv Tyler: Star in Ascendance

The Cinema of Richard Linklater

John Hughes and Eighties Cinema

Ferris Bueller's Day Off: The Pocket Movie Guide

The Christmas Movie Book

Notional Identities

The Shadow in the Gallery

The James Bond Movies of the 1980s

Mel Brooks: Genius and Loving It!

The Spectrum of Adventure

A Righteously Awesome Eighties Christmas

Contested Mindscapes

John Hughes FAQ

The Golden Age of Christmas Movies

The Heart 200 Book [with Julie Christie]

A VERY SPECTRUM CHRISTMAS

Celebrating Seasonal Software on the Sinclair ZX Spectrum

Thomas A. Christie

EXTREMIS
publishing

A Very Spectrum Christmas: Celebrating Seasonal Software on the Sinclair ZX Spectrum by Thomas A. Christie.

First edition published in Great Britain in 2021 by Extremis Publishing Ltd., Suite 218, Castle House, 1 Baker Street, Stirling, FK8 1AL, United Kingdom. *www.extremispublishing.com*

Extremis Publishing is a Private Limited Company registered in Scotland (SC509983) whose Registered Office is Suite 218, Castle House, 1 Baker Street, Stirling, FK8 1AL, United Kingdom.

A CIP catalogue record for this book is available from the British Library.

ISBN: 978-1-9996962-9-0

Typeset in Sorts Mill Goudy, designed by The League of Moveable Type.

Printed and bound in Great Britain by IngramSpark, Chapter House, Pitfield, Kiln Farm, Milton Keynes, MK11 3LW, United Kingdom.

Front cover artwork is Copyright © Maciej Duda at Shutterstock Inc. (background image) / Christos Georghiou at Shutterstock Inc. (foreground image). Back cover artwork and book spine illustration by Gerd Altmann at Pixabay.

Frontispiece artwork by Betexion at Pixabay.

Cover design and book design is Copyright © Thomas A. Christie. Incidental interior vector artwork from Pixabay.

Author images are Copyright © Julie Christie and Eddy A. Bryan.

Archive photography is sourced from the author's private collection unless otherwise stated.

CONTENTS

FOREWORD

Once upon a time, many years ago, I went to an unruly Christmas party in a very large house somewhere near Cambridge. I found sanctuary at the back of the kitchen, where I came across a lanky elf topped by shiny round spectacles. He would have had red hair if he had not embraced premature baldness. After gazing down at the floor and up at a passing bosom, he fell to talking about a forthcoming consumer opportunity for home micro computers. He told me that the purpose of home micro computers was to conduct personal accounts, solve mathematical problems and make inventories. I laughed in his face, then told him that the purpose of home micro computers was to be very silly and play games. He looked at me as if I was bonkers, which indeed I was. I confess we were more than a little drunk and in need of bladder evacuation, and when he disappeared into the toilet, I asked a passing gnome who that miserable bald bloke with shiny round specs was. "Him? Don't mind him. That's Clive Sinclair." A wee while later, the Sinclair Spectrum changed the world for everybody at that party, and a whole bunch of people beyond.

My name is Mel, and according to the history books I founded the very first videogames company in the UK. That was way back in 1977. In other words, I was a has-been before the Spectrum was a must-have. The best Christmas game I ever produced appeared on a compilation title where I modestly tried to gamify eight books of The Bible into 1K each. I called it *Bethlehem*, and I seem to remember some sort of a donkey race that involved a placenta catapult. Christmas was always a very special time for us Spectrum-mongers. We would cynically change the graphics of whatever we were working on at the time, think up a seasonal title, ramp up production for the festive season, and then miss the deadline and go back to square one. The only computing Christmas present I ever received was a law suit from Waddingtons Games concerning my Spectrum game *Go To Jail*, which involved a simulated board game of property trading. That ended up in the High Court. Waddingtons lost.

Long after I ceased to be a footnote in Spectrum gaming, I became a veteran, and eventually a legend. That's the way it goes. Such progression is easily achieved by the simple tactic of refusing to die. The problem that faces us legends is that eventually we start appearing in text books, and before you know it very nice people ask us to write forewords for their new publication. So that's how this happened.

In 2018, I turned up in an excellent book by a very fine man called Dr Thomas A Christie, all about mindscapes and dementia in modern popular culture. Tom, as I like to call him, is a big hearty Scot with teeny weeny handwriting, who once invested ten quid in one of my crowdfunders, for which I am eternally grateful. I would have gladly written this foreword for his book on the spirit of Spectrum Christmas without his tenner, but I haven't told him that. I am not doing it for the honour, and I am not doing it because I like to see my own name in print. I am doing it because Christmas is a time of forgiveness, hope and joy, and I need to write this as a confession to expiate my sin of laughing at Clive Sinclair and never thanking him for his gift to us all. So here goes ... sorry Clive, but I was right and you were wrong. Micro computers are to enable us all be very silly and play games, especially during the festive season. If you, dear reader, enjoy this book half as much as I have, then you are in for a joyous treat.

Mel Croucher
August 2021

INTRODUCTION

An incredible five million units of the Sinclair ZX Spectrum were sold, in their various different iterations, throughout the machine's 1980s heyday, and many of them were given as Christmas presents. This means that for a generation of British kids, the Spectrum will always have a special relationship with the festive season as, for many of us, it would be our first ever experience of home computer gaming.

A lot of us would spend Christmas playing games that had come with the Spectrum as gifts—maybe classics such as *Knight Lore*, *Jet Set Willy*, *Ant Attack*, or any of the other hundreds of titles which were published on the platform throughout the eighties. While that home microcomputer technology may seem primitive today, back then it was a gateway to a virtual world that was just the load of a cassette tape away.

But a Spectrum was for life, not just for Christmas, and most of us would cherish our first computers throughout the rest of the decade—sometimes even longer. Sensing a golden opportunity, many games publishers were to release yuletide-themed games year on year in the period running up to the festive season; titles which very much had Christmas traditions as their creative focus. These ran the whole gamut from text adventures to arcade action, via some truly baffling novelty titles along the way. Some were innovative, others bewildering, and a few frankly came close to defying easy categorisation altogether. But all of them have a charm that can only come from software that was written for Sir Clive Sinclair's legendary dream machine.

In this book, I'll be taking a look at many of the seasonal titles that have been produced for the Sinclair Spectrum over the years. Not just those which dealt with specifically Christmas-focused subject matter such as Santa Claus, reindeer, elves and snowmen, but other winter-themed titles which brought a bit of jollity to British homes during those long, frosty December nights. Some of these games originate from the Spectrum's 1980s glory days, while others have appeared more recently thanks to the sterling work of the machine's hugely active homebrew community across the world.

So pull up a chair, grab yourself the festive treat of your choice (a mug of hot chocolate with marshmallows is always highly recommended), and get ready for some Noël nostalgia the way only the Spectrum can present it.

The author receives his first Sinclair Spectrum, the +2A with built-in Datacorder and bundled Magnum Light Phaser, on Christmas Day 1988.

This book is dedicated to
my dear friends

Joseph and Mary Moore

The world's favourite
Santa and Mrs Claus

A VERY SPECTRUM CHRISTMAS

Celebrating Seasonal Software on the Sinclair ZX Spectrum

Thomas A. Christie

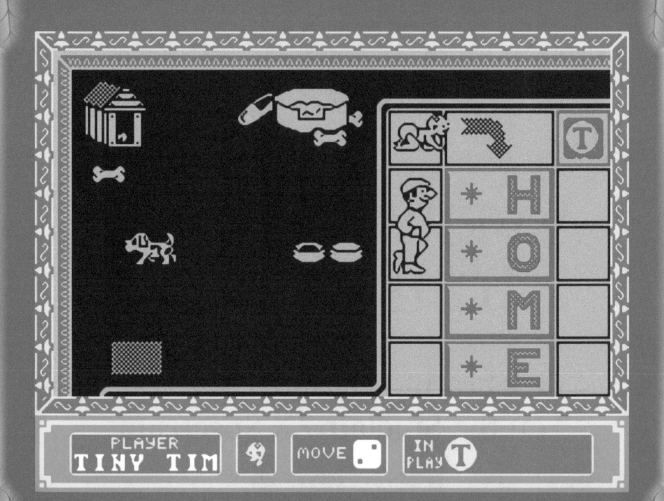

COMPENDIUM

Gremlin Graphics (1987)

Nothing speaks of the great British Christmas quite like gathering the family around a traditional board game, then rapidly descending into an inevitable argument (and quite possibly a mind-boggling amount of cheating) as dice are feverishly rolled after a glass of port or two. In 1987, Sheffield-based software titans Gremlin Graphics—one of the most iconic British software publishers active in the world of 1980s computing, which had previously unleashed cult classics such as *Jack the Nipper* (1986) and *Wanted: Monty Mole* (1984) onto an unsuspecting world—made the intriguing decision to take this venerable post-Queen's Speech activity by the scruff of the neck and cast it headlong into the digital age.

Compendium was a cheerful compilation of four time-honoured kids' games, each of them given an eighties makeover. The eponymous tetralogy consisted of *Snakes and Hazards* (a variation on snakes and ladders), *X-Mas Ludo* (the halcyon game of ludo with a festive twist), *Shove a Sledge* (an updating of shove ha'penny) and *Tiddly Drinks* (a very loose adaptation of tiddlywinks). While there was a degree of variety in the gameplay across each of the titles, visual commonality was retained from game to game thanks to a shared pool of characters—the suitably jolly Wink family, which included the permanently tipsy Tiddly Wink, his long-suffering wife Mavis, teenage kids Ralph and Victoria, infant Tiny Tim and dog Sniffer.

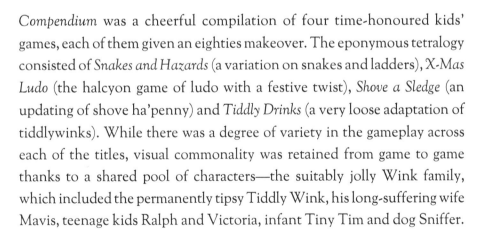

Various playable selections of the characters appear in each of the compilation's games, and each had their own signature theme; Sniffer always

appears to the sound of Bob Merrill's '(How Much is) That Doggy in the Window?' (1952), for instance, while Victoria is accompanied by the Charlie Rich song 'The Most Beautiful Girl' (1973). The large sprites are suitably detailed, ranging from the bespectacled Ralph to the nappy-clad Tiny Tim via Tiddly Wink with his trademark beer belly, but what truly lends character to each family member is each of their unique individual foibles which are revealed as the games unfold.

Each game has a surprise element or two up its sleeve. While *Snakes and Hazards* operates along similar lines to the original game, where players can ascend ladders or slide down snakes depending on whether the dice falls in their favour, the characters can be distracted by particular diversions which cause them to stray from the task at hand. If Victoria encounters a telephone (a landline, naturally— this was the eighties, after all), she can't resist calling her friends for a chat, while the studious Ralph is unable to ignore any pile of books that might appear in his path. Adding to the challenge are non-player characters who can push the player out of their square, and slightly more outlandish figures such as mutant holly plant Shady Leaf and rampaging Christmas pudding Meanus Puddus who are also on hand, determined to grind proceedings to a standstill. Nonetheless,

everyone's familiarity with the game's simple goal of reaching the hundredth square before the other players does at least mean that *Snakes and Hazards* is suitably intuitive to pick up and play.

X-Mas Ludo is played in a very similar fashion, this time (as the name suggests) following the rules of ludo in that each player must make their way around the board four times if they are to reach the safety of 'home' while avoiding the Wink parents, who are patrolling the board with the intent of stopping their progress. In *Shove a Sledge*, Tiny Tim

2

needs the help of one of the other characters to be pushed along an icy slide on his sledge; successful players will push the toddler just hard enough to land between particular dividing lines, while dodging Sniffer's attempts to derail their efforts. Finally, Tiddly Wink takes centre stage in *Tiddly Drinks*, where the inebriated patriarch has assumed residence in his local pub. After downing a pint of beer (or six), he inexplicably decides to throw each glass into the air, leaving his family scrambling around to catch the errant projectile before it can hit the floor and smash into smithereens. The winner is the character who is able to catch the greatest amount of glassware while it remains intact.

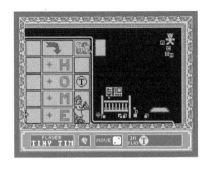

Reviewers of the time were deeply sceptical of *Compendium*'s merits. While many commentators praised the distinctive characters, the game's offbeat sense of humour and the tongue-in-cheek music cues (at least on the 128K version of the game), there was a general sense that computerising board games had been a somewhat superfluous endeavour. Surely if the best thing about a traditional board game is its ability to get friends and family around the coffee table to share each other's company, playing one on a computer negates (or at the very least dilutes) the appeal somewhat? The rather sluggish movement of the characters—especially when there are a few figures in motion at the same time—also came in for criticism, while lethargic scrolling slowed the gameplay.

With its ebullient range of Christmas carols and a decidedly cosy ambiance, *Compendium* retains considerable charm when played around the festive season. From its onscreen rolling dice to the pleasingly eccentric cast of characters, the game exhibited plenty of the presentational polish that Gremlin Graphics was famous for. While it may never be the first title people are inclined to think of when considering the publisher's celebrated output, it is nonetheless a fun diversion which benefits greatly from its *Everyone's a Wally*-style ensemble line-up. Even those who are immune to its charms may still find themselves yearning for a simpler age of draughts and dominoes.

SANTA'S CHRISTMAS CAPERS

Zeppelin Games (1991)

Perhaps the most immediately-recognisable icon of the modern festive season, Santa Claus received his fair share of yuletide appearances on the Sinclair Spectrum—some better received than others. Arriving in the early 1990s, near the end of the machine's original lifespan, *Santa's Christmas Capers* has become one of the most infamous games to feature the red-suited chimney diver and his Christmas Eve gift distribution practices.

Zeppelin Games was a well-known software publisher on the 8-bit computer scene between the late eighties and early nineties, and were responsible for a number of popular releases including *Bionic Commando* (1989), *Sharkey's Moll* (1991) and *Match of the Day* (1992), alongside rather more eccentric fare such as *Blinky's Scary School* (1990), *Phileas Fogg's Balloon Battles* (1991) and *Sleepwalker* (1992). *Santa's Christmas Capers*—also sometimes known by its working title *You Are Santa Claus*—definitely fell more towards the offbeat end of their release slate.

According to the instructions, Santa has been taken out of commission by rebellious elves from his workshop, meaning that the player must take his place if the children of the world are to receive their festive gifts as normal. The game was a horizontally-scrolling shoot-'em-up (think along the lines of a bargain counter version of *R-Type* with added figgy pudding) in which the player—in the guise of a substitute Santa—must race through the skies in their sleigh, firing like crazy at oncoming hazards such as Christmas crackers, rubber bath ducks, toy trains, penguins and plungers as they collect a range of wine glasses and bobble-hatted Santa heads in mid-air. Setting off from the workshop in Lapland, the stand-in Santa must battle first through the North Pole and then over the Atlantic Ocean (where their sleigh must dodge radar waves, amongst other obstacles, to evade detection) before arriving on dry land, at which point the goal switches from gathering presents to delivering them. The player must drop gifts from Santa's sleigh down the chimneys of passing houses while avoiding yet more oncoming dangers—including unwanted presents from the year beforehand. Here the plot thickens: the treacherous elves aim to disrupt Christmas so that they no longer need to spend all year manufacturing new toys and, to this end, have distributed plum pudding bombs around the level in the hope of disrupting Santa's deliveries. Can the locum jolly old St Nick clear a path through the explosives to save Christmas in time for the big day?

Santa's Christmas Capers was universally panned by the industry press of the time, with criticism directed at the odd perspective of the action (Santa and his sleigh seem tiny, while the other sprites appear oversized by comparison), repetitive plinky-plonk musical rendition of 'We Wish You a Merry Christmas', the flickery motion and confusing degree of sprite overlap. While the characters are large and colourful, movement is frequently jerky and the action lacks variety. Similarly, there is not much of a defined difficulty curve, with the bewildering array of onrushing threats (and their attendant colour clash) seeming oddly random from moment to moment. There is plenty of jollity in the presentation of *Santa's Christmas Capers*, from the sprigs of holly surrounding the player's score through to the seasonal snowmen and fir trees of the North Pole, but sadly there is not nearly as much joy to be experienced in actually playing the game itself.

THE WHITE DOOR

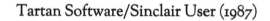

Tartan Software/Sinclair User (1987)

While the festive season may seem to lend itself most obviously to colourful action games, Christmas has also made an appearance in a surprising number of text adventures over the years. Among the most atmospheric of these interaction fiction titles was *The White Door*, otherwise known as *Crisis at Christmas*, which first appeared in issue 58 of *Sinclair User*—the festive special edition of the magazine, released in time for Christmas 1986.

The White Door was created by prolific adventure game writer Tom Frost, who subsequently released it on his Tartan Software label along with other instalments in the *Doors* series which ran between 1987 and 1988 and comprised the thematically-linked *The Open Door*, *The Green Door*, *The Red Door* and *The Yellow Door*. Tartan Software was based in Montrose in the beautiful Scottish county of Angus, and Frost produced many popular and well-received interactive fiction titles for the Spectrum which included *1942 Mission* (1984), *Double Agent* (1987) and *The Gordello Incident* (1989).

The game's action takes place late on Christmas Eve in the English city of Milton Keynes. It is half-past nine at night, a blizzard is raging, and the player arrives home at their snow-covered 'white house' only to immediately be tasked with tracking down, wrapping and carefully positioning two errant festive gifts for their character's children John and Clare in order to ensure that all goes smoothly on Christmas morning. In a pleasing (if relatively unusual) twist for the time, the game offered a choice of protagonists—players could select either husband Ron or wife Nancy (calling to mind an entirely different White House of the 1980s!)—though both are charged with the same responsibility: to make sure that everything is in place for the family before the big day ahead.

The White Door exhibits not just an abundance of Frost's quick wit, but also his talent for creating a believable and distinctive playing environment. Finding a couple of Christmas presents might not seem like the most high-stakes goal ever to appear in a text adventure game, but—thanks to the wintry, late night ambiance that is carefully generated in the early scenes—an unmistakable sense of yuletide urgency is gradually evoked as the main character becomes ever more aware of the need to uncover the missing gifts and get them into place in time for the coming day's unwrapping session. The limited number of locations within the house also creates a sense of snug Christmas Eve tranquillity, with snow piling down outside and a need to explore every nook and cranny of this inviting family home in order to find the necessary items—which, as it turns out, includes a few more surprises than just the misplaced gifts.

While the mystery presents are perhaps not quite as startling as you might hope or expect when they do finally turn up, there are still more than a few convolutions involved in pinpointing them—though the greatest challenge of all might be the unforgiving inventory system, which enables the character to carry only a strictly limited number of items at a time. Given the need to wrap the gifts as well as initially finding them, this leads to a fair amount of object manipulation as certain items are discovered only for the player to be forced to drop them again in order to carry other things in their place. (This, in turn, means that they will need to be relocated later in the game, so careful placement proves to be important.) Likewise, while the game's command prompt employed the usual 'verb-noun' combinations the parser can be surprisingly demanding at times; having found

batteries for a torch, the player should conserve power wherever possible in case they need to use it later, but the commands 'turn off torch' or 'switch off torch' aren't recognised—only 'extinguish torch' will do the trick. A few other syntactic and logical intricacies must be disentangled before the game is completed, not least a less-than-intuitive way of discovering the house's loft hatch and a curious method of impersonating Santa Claus with the aid of a red poncho and shaving cream. After all, how can you deliver presents on Christmas Eve without a visit from Father Christmas himself—or, at the very least, a reasonably close approximation?

Though *The White Door* may not be the most challenging adventure that Frost ever wrote, it certainly exuded plenty of charm for players looking to while away an hour or two over the festive season. Perhaps most importantly, although neither the lost gifts nor their locations were particularly unanticipated (not just for stalwart text adventure fans, but for anyone with even a passing familiarity with the popular culture of the time), any lapse in originality can be forgiven on account of the head-scratching mystification caused by the game's modest but obscure range of puzzles. Anyone who has ever found themselves rummaging around in a garden shed in a December blizzard desperately searching for a mislaid gift will be right at home with this offbeat scenario of seasonal domestic quandaries.

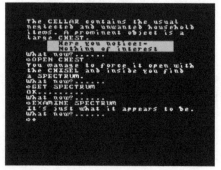

Tom Frost continued to produce interactive fiction into the 1990s, but the wide distribution of *The White Door* alongside *Sinclair User* meant that the title has come to be one of his best-remembered and most widely-played games. Although it admittedly may not be his most taxing title, there is still no small amount of festive allure on display—not least for anyone who grew up during the eighties and who feels nostalgic for Christmas customs of the recent past. As text adventures go, it remains as inviting as a glass of mulled wine and a warm fireplace.

COMPUTER CHRISTMAS CARD

Virgin Games (1985)

One of the greatest Christmas curios to appear on the Spectrum was the unusual attempt by Virgin Games to supplant the venerable Christmas card with a computerised version, which appeared at the budget price of £2.99 back in 1985. The computer magazines of the time were somewhat sceptical of this development, considering it a rather cynical cash-in which was unlikely to challenge the ubiquity of the physical greetings cards popularised by Sir Henry Cole from 1843 onwards.

The program itself was straightforward. The user was asked to enter the name of the person the card is intended for, and then to enter their own name so that the recipient would know who had sent it. There followed a short medley of Christmas carols (rendered in all the bleepy glory that the Spectrum's sound chip was renowned for) before a brief scene played out which saw Santa arriving on a rooftop, descending the chimney, and proceeding to fill the Christmas stockings of the unsuspecting householders prior to helping himself to a glass of sherry on the way back to his sleigh. Providing a bit of extra value for money, a distinctly non-festive shoot-'em-up entitled *Space Command* could be found on the cassette's B-side.

Sending your Christmas cards on a Spectrum cassette tape never did catch on or supersede their paper-based equivalent in the eighties, but many other variants on the concept would follow in later years—and in some ways, the whole idea was arguably just a decade or so ahead of its time, foreshadowing the e-mail greetings cards that so many of us receive over the Internet from friends and relatives in the present day.

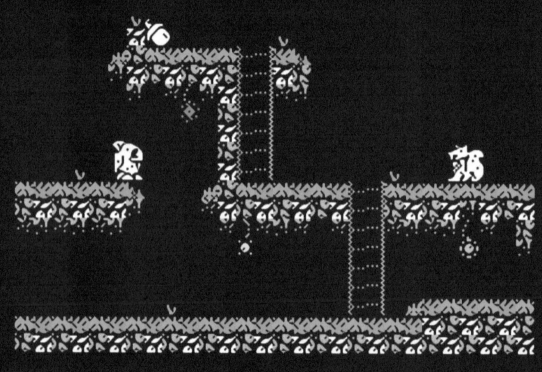

TOOFY'S WINTER NUTS

Paul Jenkinson (2013)

In spite of their immediate association with the golden age of home computing, Spectrum games aren't just the domain of the 1980s and early '90s. Thanks to the sterling efforts of independent developers the world over, new titles have emerged for Sir Clive Sinclair's wonder machine even in recent years, and Christmas games are no exception. One of the more distinctive figures to emerge from this thriving homebrew scene is Toofy, the brainchild of Paul Jenkinson, who has been the star of a number of platform games including *Toofy in Fan Land* (2012) and *Toofy's Nutty Nightmare* (2020). In 2012, however, the character made a rather more seasonal appearance in the commendably silly *Toofy's Winter Nuts*.

Perhaps first and foremost, the question has to be asked... exactly what is Toofy actually supposed to be? Apart from a single, protruding tooth (from which his name presumably derives), his only defining characteristic appears to be his singular obsession with collecting nuts—and yet, should anyone be inclined to think that he is possibly a very oddly-shaped squirrel, this theory is promptly torpedoed by the fact that the unlikely adversaries of *Toofy's Winter Nuts* are... a gang of kleptomaniac squirrels, much more recognisably rendered, who are conspiring to steal the nuts of the title. So it seems that we must be content with the explanation that he is simply an unknown creature of unspecified origins—albeit one with a clear mission: namely to liberate his food supplies from the bushy-tailed villains seeking to purloin them from right under his (vaguely-defined) nose.

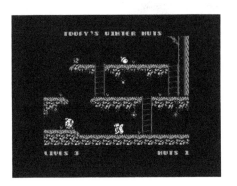

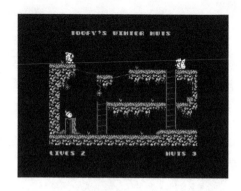

The game's action has much in common with many classic platform games of yesteryear, including *Chuckie Egg II* (1985) and *Auf Wiedersehen Monty* (1987), in that Toofy must make his way across a landscape riddled with hazards, dodging squirrels and any other obstacles, as he collects as many nuts as he can. The ultimate objective is to gather enough of the scattered food to last all winter once it is safely stored in Toofy's den. The game follows a more or less linear path (albeit with a few diversions here and there), with ladders on the various screens allowing the character to ascend or descend to dodge hostiles and access out-of-reach targets with the aid of platforms. The bad news is that the squirrels can climb the ladders too, though with a well-timed jump Toofy can still manage to circumvent their approach. In each level, trapdoors lead further down into subterranean zones once a necessary number of nuts have been gathered, granting access to slightly different playing areas.

Jenkinson produced the game with the use of Jonathan Cauldwell's acclaimed *Arcade Games Designer* (2008) creation package, and *Toofy's Winter Nuts* is an excellent demonstration of what this well-regarded utility is capable of. Toofy is a gleefully characterful sprite, full of lopsided charm, and the game marked a major shift up in gear from its warmly-received predecessor *Toofy in Fan Land*, seeming more polished and refined all round. Like the best platform games, no complex plot is required—simply reuniting the hapless Toofy with his pilfered nuts is more than enough to get the action started—and everything oozes appealing quirkiness from the cheeky (if light-fingered) squirrels roaming around the platforms through to the colourful playing environment. With over thirty individual screens, there is plenty of exploring to be done, and the action is sped up by flipping between adjacent screens rather than attempting to scroll from one location to another.

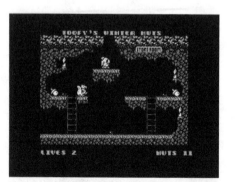

The game's difficulty level is carefully pitched, with things becoming decidedly trickier the further underground Toofy manages to progress. Timing becomes ever more important if enemies are to be avoided (the collision detection is thankfully very well-judged, avoiding frustration), and some jumps have to be pixel-perfect if the player is to carry them off successfully. Thankfully the gameplay never becomes so fiddly that exasperation starts to set in, and just the right element of challenge is required to progress through the levels. Toofy is given a reasonably generous number of lives (by platform game standards, at any rate) at the start of the game, which is just as well as the movement of the squirrels doesn't follow a set pattern, but instead their motions contain an element of randomness which means that the player has to anticipate their next move.

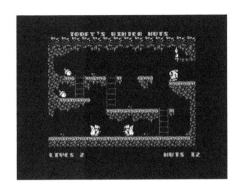

Toofy's Winter Nuts may not be the all-out tinsel and cracker-bedecked yuletide assault on the senses that some other festive games offer, but it is nonetheless a pleasant modern addition to the platform action game genre which provides a likeable central figure, an enjoyable escapade and plenty of playability. Paul Jenkinson has made many contributions to Spectrum software over the past decade or so, ranging from text adventures such as *A Broken Friend* (2012) and *The Firm* (2016) to *Thrust*-style action game *Space Disposal* (2011) and *Airwolf*-inspired helicopter game *Chopper Drop* (2011). It is, however, for his many platform games that he is most likely to be known, with charmingly tongue-in-cheek adventures such as *Antiquity Jones* (2012), *Baldy ZX* (2015) and *Code Zero* (2017) all proving that there is most definitely still plenty of life left in the Spectrum even in the present day. *Toofy's Winter Nuts* may have been a rare sidestep into the world of seasonal fare compared to his well-stocked back catalogue, but Jenkinson was also to have another—decidedly more festively-themed—title up his sleeve which would emerge some years later...

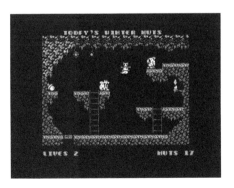

THE SNOWMAN

Quicksilva (1984)

For generations of British children, Raymond Briggs' *The Snowman* has been a beloved Christmas TV tradition. First broadcast on Channel Four on Boxing Day 1982, the animation—based on Briggs' award-winning 1978 illustrated storybook of the same name—immediately won a legion of fans due to its beautiful evocation of a snowy Christmas Eve, its astonishing Howard Blake soundtrack, and the haunting central song 'Walking in the Air' which was performed to great acclaim by chorister Peter Auty. (It became even more famous three years later when it was recorded by Aled Jones, reaching #5 in the UK charts.) *The Snowman* was nominated for an Academy Award and won numerous other industry awards, eventually inspiring a number of spin-off productions including a stage show and live concert. With annual screenings on Channel Four every Christmas (now accompanied by its similarly-beguiling sequel, 2012's *The Snowman and the Snowdog*), *The Snowman* has continued to be a staple of the British festive season ever since, but its computer adaptation has remained comparatively little-known following its release in 1984.

Published by Southampton-based software house Quicksilva, *The Snowman* on the Spectrum was a suitably colourful affair—and while no attempt is made to follow the plotline of the TV animation (where a young boy discovers that his snowman has magically come to life on the night of Christmas Eve, and flies with him all the way to the North Pole to meet Father Christmas), the game retains the allure of the Briggs original by recreating the very essence of the story: the creation of the famous

An enchanting Christmas game based on RAYMOND BRIGGS' best selling book and film.

The Snowman is Copyright © Penguin Ventures/Raymond Briggs

Snowman himself. The player takes the role of the unnamed boy, who must first construct the body of the Snowman and then add items of clothing such as his trademark scarf and hat.

To complete this task, the youthful protagonist must make his way around the paths of his home's garden, collecting everything he will need to build the Snowman in time for his frozen friend to come to life. There are various dangers to outmanoeuvre along the way, including 'sleep monsters' which must be neutralised by an alarm clock, moving gas flames which can be frozen in place using an ice lolly, and of course good old-fashioned fatigue which can be staved off by eating festive food items (such as Christmas pudding) scattered around the playing area. If the unnamed youngster should lose all of his lives, he will end up fast asleep in bed—thus missing out on his annual Christmas Eve adventures with his snowy chum.

The Snowman does an admirable job of reconstructing the gentle charm of the Briggs book, and the simple platform-based approach (moving up and down ramps which represent garden paths) is straightforward for players of all ages. Sadly none of the Howard Blake music was recomposed for the Spectrum release, though there were a few Christmas tunes in evidence between levels (the game has four sections, each with a slightly different layout) to provide some degree of musical accompaniment.

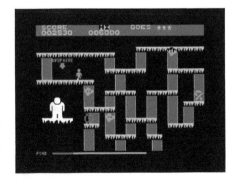

Though the company may well be forever remembered best for their pioneering isometric action game *Ant Attack* (1983), Quicksilva would later produce numerous popular titles for the Spectrum including *Glider Rider* (1986), *Max Headroom* (1986) and *Elevator Action* (1986). *The Snowman* was warmly received by many critics of the time, with reviews highlighting its nonviolent action, detailed and recognisable Snowman character as he slowly takes form, and cross-generational appeal. Like the animation which inspired it, *The Snowman* is an appealing slice of Christmas entertainment.

PLUM DUFF

00009

Dashing through the snow on a one-horse open sleigh.

Please Santa, could you bring me a paintbox or some crayons. O. Frey.

PLUM DUFF

Bug-Byte Software (1985)

It's a disaster at Christmas! Jolly Old Saint Nick, having had one too many glasses of sherry, has accidentally delivered gifts to the wrong houses. Now he has no choice but to revisit all of the homes in the affected street in order to track down the wayward presents and make sure that they are returned to their rightful place. But with no less than 32 kids in the area, all of whom are watching avidly for the merest glimpse of a red suit on the night of Christmas Eve, Santa will have his work cut out to collect all of the gifts and rearrange their destinations without being rumbled.

Following a passably jaunty rendition of 'Away in a Manger' and some very respectable synthesised speech, it's straight into the action as Santa flies over the rooftops in his reindeer-drawn sleigh while trying to avoid a collision with some seemingly-random objects in midair. This horizontally-scrolling section of the game is little more than a brief diversion for Father Christmas to make his way from one property to another as he traverses the street. Should he strike a chimney stack, however, he will find himself magically transported into the home beneath—and into the thick of the action, as from this point on the game takes the form of a *Pyjamarama*-style arcade adventure in a cosy domestic setting.

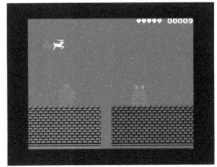

Santa must make his way around each house (his task made more difficult by the fact that many of them seem very similar in their contents and layout), picking up presents by use of the fire button and then depositing them in the right stocking. To aid his efforts, a panel on the bottom-right of the screen displays each child's letter to Santa asking for a particular

17

present which enables him to put each gift in the correct place. Appearing on the bottom-left panel, by comparison, is a seemingly endless series of Christmas cracker jokes and other witty, festively-themed asides (some admittedly more amusing than others).

While Santa's mission may seem straightforward enough, if a child should spot him then they will immediately race to his side which inevitably causes problems and leaves Saint Nick with no option but to retreat or else find a hiding place such as a nearby wardrobe. Other hazards include inexplicably deadly pot-plants which, if encountered, will sap Santa's energy even further and put his gift-rearrangement activities in jeopardy.

For all its undeniable appeal, *Plum Duff* quickly begins to feel repetitive on account of the similarity of its environments—because the household objects and furniture are reused from home to home in order to conserve memory, it can sometimes be difficult to know initially whether Santa is visiting a particular property for a second time, leading to a definite sense of deja-vu. (The addition of different Christmas decorations in each of the homes is a nice touch, however.) Likewise, the limited range of hazards adds to the general sense of 'sameyness' which permeates proceedings, undermining the game's genuinely fun central concept.

Plum Duff was one of the quirkiest titles to be released by Bug-Byte Software, whose releases included political strategy simulator *General Election* (1983), space-based strategy game *Star Trader* (1984), and atmospheric text adventure *Twin Kingdom Valley* (1984) amongst many others. The game's talented programmer, Jas C. Brooke, would go on to develop a versatile range of titles in later years such as gambling simulator *Miami Dice* (1986), inventive puzzle game *Rasterscan* (1987), and comic strip tie-in *Andy Capp* (1988). As Christmas games go, however, *Plum Duff* was ultimately fated to be more of a stocking filler than a centrepiece present.

FIVE RINGS

Chip Fork (2019)

Nothing whatsoever to do with the Olympics, marks left on desks by coffee cups, nor even what you give your parents on the phone to let them know that you've got home safely, *Five Rings* by Simon Daly is described on the title screen (with much tongue-in-cheek charm) as a 'vaguely interactive Crimble ghost story' which operates along similar lines to the style of choose-your-own-adventure games popularised by titles such as Creative Sparks' much-loved 1984 illustrated interactive fiction title *Danger Mouse in the Black Forest Chateau* and Mosaic Software's fondly-remembered home computer adaptation of Sue Townsend's *The Secret Diary of Adrian Mole Aged 13¾* (1985).

The game first appeared on *WOOT! Tape Magazine*'s third issue (the 'ZXmas' 2019 edition), and eschewed a traditional text adventure parser in favour of a much simpler interface which invites the player to influence the action by choosing between options at particular junctures when prompted. This straightforward method of interaction makes the game very accessible, particularly for causal gamers. The narrative is described via scrolling text at the top of the screen, with action prompts appearing at the bottom and a changing graphical illustration in the centre.

The story of *Five Rings* was as atmospheric as it was efficiently told. Heading home after work on a day just before Christmas, the protagonist decides to take a brief detour through a nearby village where they had fond memories of growing up. Though they no longer have any surviving relatives there, the trip offers up a little seasonal nostalgia. However, this

sentimental journey is interrupted when a fox suddenly appears in the road, causing the unnamed driver to either swerve or slam on the brakes. From there, the player's character decides to stay in the village for a while to calm their nerves, leading indirectly to a mystery involving a missing professor, some nearby ancient standing stones which bear a strange symbol (the mysterious five rings of the title), and a recently-uncovered Sinclair Spectrum cassette from the eighties which might just be more than it seems at face value. But when they are invited to the village's annual midnight flambeau festival, focusing on the aforementioned neolithic monument, there is an ominous suspicion that things may not end well...

With its stylised, minimalist illustrations and moody blue-and-green palette, the game certainly conjures an impressively dark, crepuscular ambiance throughout, though this is counterbalanced by the author's droll line in observational wit which means that the story never drifts too far into the realms of conventional horror territory. Given the nature of the multiple choice interface, *Five Rings* has a degree of replay value in the sense that players can approach the narrative a few times to try alternative options and witness the way in which their decisions alter the flow of the plot.

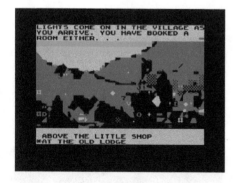

Five Rings offers only a short playing experience, but one which evocatively captures the spirit of a traditional Christmas ghost story. With its sly subversion of that most central trope of the festive season—the giving and receiving of gifts—it neatly subverts expectation not just of the supernatural tale but also of its yuletide setting. The game is inventive without being revolutionary, easy to pick up and play, and presents the perfect diversion for a chilly winter's night in the approach to Christmas. It even comes with a moral for the ages: if you should happen to encounter a fox on its hind legs offering you an unexpected present in the dead of night then, in the grand tradition of *Grange Hill*, always be prepared to 'just say no'.

MOLEY CHRISTMAS

Gremlin Graphics/Your Sinclair (1987)

Nothing says Christmas like an affable subterranean mammal, and Monty Mole was one of the biggest stars of the Sinclair Spectrum; a home-grown hero created by Pete Harrap for Gremlin Graphics' controversial, miners' strike-inspired platform game *Wanted: Monty Mole* (1984). The great British public took Monty to their hearts, and he eventually became as synonymous with the 8-bit computer scene as figures such as Miner Willy, Dizzy and Jack the Nipper, meaning that the diminutive short-sighted character soon featured in further titles including *Monty is Innocent* (1985), *Monty on the Run* (1985) and *Auf Wiedersehen Monty* (1987).

It was with much fanfare that the popular (and ever-irreverent) *Your Sinclair* magazine unveiled that they would be featuring a special exclusive in their Christmas issue for 1987; Monty would be making an appearance (hyped for some time beforehand) on their covermount cassette tape in a brand new festive adventure. Such was the eponymous mole's cult credentials by this time, the news was met with much enthusiasm by eighties gamers eager to see their favourite tunnelling rodent back in action once again.

The game wisely refuses to complicate the winning platform action of the previous Monty titles, with our furry hero jumping and climbing between levels as he goes about a variety of tasks. In a fourth-wall-breaking twist, the objective of *Moley Christmas* is to produce the very game that the user is playing. Thus the first section involves Monty picking up the code for the game from the Gremlin Graphics office, the second sees him dropping it off at a cassette mastering plant and collecting the resulting mastertape,

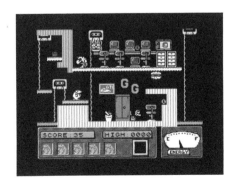

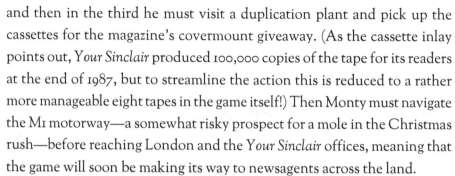

and then in the third he must visit a duplication plant and pick up the cassettes for the magazine's covermount giveaway. (As the cassette inlay points out, *Your Sinclair* produced 100,000 copies of the tape for its readers at the end of 1987, but to streamline the action this is reduced to a rather more manageable eight tapes in the game itself!) Then Monty must navigate the M1 motorway—a somewhat risky prospect for a mole in the Christmas rush—before reaching London and the *Your Sinclair* offices, meaning that the game will soon be making its way to newsagents across the land.

The action of *Moley Christmas* is most reminiscent of its two immediate predecessors, *Monty on the Run* and *Auf Wiedersehen Monty* (reusing the Ben Daglish music from the latter on the 128K version), so gamers would find much that was familiar. Naturally there is the expected plethora of surreal obstacles to avoid if Monty is to succeed in his quest (some will deplete his energy level while others will cause him to lose a life), and there are plenty of clever incidental details to spot. With only six playable screens, it lacks the longevity of Monty's rather more ambitious commercial outings, and in truth is more of a novelty than a full-blown platform adventure.

It is, however, easy to overlook just how huge an event this was for *Your Sinclair*; the magazine trailed the game in the previous month's issue, and the resulting reader interest paved the way for further promotional exclusives of a similar nature from other software developers in the years that followed. The staff even organised a prize competition to coincide with the game's appearance; the first person to send in the text from the congratulations screen at the conclusion won no less than fifteen Spectrum games.

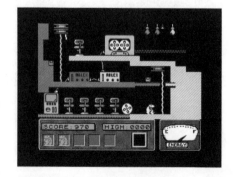

In spite of *Your Sinclair* heralding this as the last ever Monty Mole game, the character would go on to make one further appearance on the Spectrum in the superhero-themed *Impossamole* (1990). But while *Moley Christmas* may not be Monty's best-known outing, it was certainly an enjoyable festive adventure for the character that never outstays its welcome.

PERCY PENGUIN IN THE PRESENT PALAVER

Snagultoof (2019)

Penguins are so often the unsung heroes of Christmas-themed games: usually reindeers and polar bears take centre stage when it comes to animals that are associated with the festive season. But the plucky Percy was soon to rectify that injustice, and prove once and for all that small flightless birds were just as capable of saving Christmas as anyone else.

In an unfortunate mishap as he sets off on his yearly deliveries, Santa accidentally drops a number of gifts from his sleigh which land far below in the foreboding icicle forest. As the elves have all gone home for the holidays, it falls to Percy the helpful penguin to retrieve all of the errant presents and return them to Santa within an hour if he is to avoid seeing Christmas put in jeopardy.

Percy Penguin in the Present Palaver is a platform-based item collection game which is very much in the style of old favourites such as Software Projects' *Jet Set Willy* (1984) and Hewson Consultants' *Technician Ted* (1984). Though—like others of his species—Percy lacks the power of flight, he does at least have a pair of ice skates which he can use to slide left and right, and can jump just high enough to avoid the marauding creatures trying to hamper his gift-recovery efforts. And as it happens, the forest contains no

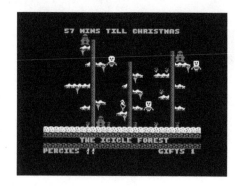

shortage of wildlife: squirrels, snowy owls, polar bears and many other denizens prowl the surroundings in a general attempt to get in Percy's way.

Created with the use of Jonathan Cauldwell's *Arcade Games Designer*, the game provides quite a challenge; there is an expansive playing area, the time limit adds to the pressure, and while the collision detection is well-judged the player must be sure to make some pretty accurate jumps if they are to avoid Percy falling foul of his woodland foes. However, where the game really shines is in its unabashed eccentricity. The title screen is accompanied by a rather jaunty rendition of that 'traditional yuletide melody', Robert Folk's instantly-recognisable theme tune to eighties comedy classic *Police Academy* (1984), and the action just gets more surreal from there.

With a healthy number of lives at his disposal, Percy has to unleash some serious penguin ingenuity if he is to collect all of the lost gifts—some of which have landed in fiendishly hard-to-reach places. The presents include plenty of nostalgic goodies from pop culture past, including Space Hoppers, Nintendo Gameboys, Etch-a-Sketches, Stylophones, Rubik's Cubes, Mr Frosty ice makers and even toy replicas of Percy himself. This cornucopia of Christmas present history from recent decades is easily one of *Percy Penguin*'s most appealing features, and the ingenuity—both in game design and the entertaining choice of collectable objectives—elevates the game beyond many of its competitors.

Demonstrating an exultantly goofy sense of humour and with a perfectly-pitched difficulty level, it would be very hard to dislike *Percy Penguin and the Present Palaver*. It displays an obvious affection for the festive season, and wears its heart on its sleeve both as a tribute to Spectrum games of the eighties as much as to the must-have Christmas presents of bygone decades.

57 MINS TILL CHRISTMAS

FROSTY ARE THE SNOWMEN

PERCIES 🐧🐧🐧   GIFTS 3

SUMMER SANTA

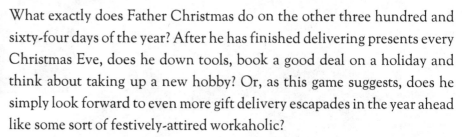

Alpha-Omega Software (1986)

What exactly does Father Christmas do on the other three hundred and sixty-four days of the year? After he has finished delivering presents every Christmas Eve, does he down tools, book a good deal on a holiday and think about taking up a new hobby? Or, as this game suggests, does he simply look forward to even more gift delivery escapades in the year ahead like some sort of festively-attired workaholic?

Created by John Hopper (who had previously produced the arcade maze game *The Life of Harry* for Cascade Games in 1985), *Summer Santa* featured box art which proudly presented Santa in a swimming costume, bobbing around on an inflatable as he suns himself at the beach. Alas, the summer-time theme ends there, for even the instructions make no reference to the unseasonal time of year which supposedly marks the game's setting.

Kicking off with a decidedly monotonic musical rendering of 'Ding Dong Merrily on High' (or some variation thereof), Santa finds himself in his grotto where he must collect one single gift at a time from his box of toys and deliver it to various recipients in a house while they sleep—save for the property's owner himself, who must be avoided lest Santa's cover be blown. Succeed, and he can collect another gift and start the whole process again. When out and about, Jolly Old Saint Nick will meet with various hazards including barking dogs and attacking birds, though perhaps the greatest danger to his safety comes from the dodgy collision detection which means that every jump is potentially a highly unpredictable prospect.

The main Santa sprite also has a tendency to flicker when moving, which can eventually have a distinctly headache-inducing effect on the player.

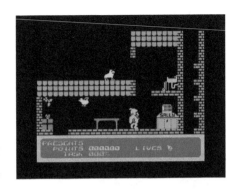

There are a few nice details on display—a TV aerial on the roof, kitchen appliances coming to life after dark (*Poltergeist*-style), and cobwebs in the cellar—but sadly these charming touches were never quite enough to make up for the numerous gameplay frustrations. Even at its £1.99 budget price point, *Summer Santa* offered little variety, and a very restrictive playing area of just eight screens. There were also some baffling design decisions, such as Santa arriving on the roof of the house only to land in the midst of two angry dogs; with no space to jump, he must move right immediately or expend all five of his lives in short order. Thankfully the copious amounts of sherry that he drinks along the way (collecting every glass leads to an increase in his total score) has no deleterious effect on his co-ordination.

Perhaps the most baffling aspect of the game was the complete avoidance of its central premise: were it not for the title and cover artwork that was suggestive of a heatwave, *Summer Santa* contains no reference whatever to midsummer sunshine, and the action could just as easily have played out in any usual Christmas Eve scenario common to Santa Claus-themed games. This led most reviewers in the trade press to reflect on whether the game hadn't quite been completed in time for a festive season release, and had instead been brought out in the height of summer in the hope that the unusually incongruous gimmick would raise its profile.

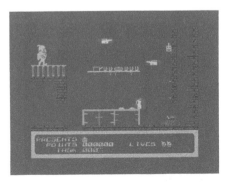

Reviews of the game generally rated it from poor to mediocre, with some faint praise for the straightforward plotline and puzzle elements, but an overall sense that the game failed to capitalise on its clever concept. Alpha-Omega Software produced some intriguing titles in its time, such as text adventure *Custerd's Quest* (1986) and innovative 3D maze game *Deathball 2000* (1986). Sadly, *Summer Santa* wasn't one of their best efforts.

WINTER TERM

Alfo Software (1989)

Winter in Britain isn't just about Christmas crackers and mince pies. It can also involve freezing cold weather, driving rain, and a depressingly lengthy queue in shopping centres alongside people with seriously frayed tempers. It's this under-explored aspect of the festive experience in the UK that is epitomised by the rather enigmatic *Winter Term*.

Game designers Alan D. Lomer and F. O'Toole, who worked together on sports management simulator *Boxing Coach* and text adventure title *On the Run* in the same year for Alfo Software, produced this thoroughly offbeat slice of interactive fiction in which the unnamed main character is forced to trek around their town in search of some money-making opportunities. The reason for this unusually down-to-earth quest is that, for unknown reasons, the protagonist owes his mother £50 and has been told in no uncertain terms that he will not be allowed home until he has repaid her in full. There's only one problem: they don't have a penny to their name, and must devise some fairly convoluted schemes fast if they are to generate the necessary cash to get out of the freezing wind and rain.

As the title suggests, the protagonist is a high school pupil—hence their permanently cash-strapped status—and while the game accurately reflects the dreariness of a wet December in an unknown and unspecified provincial British town, its action is really little more than a thin excuse to lampoon the UK social mores of the time. Programmed with the aid of Incentive Software's halcyon *The Graphic Adventure Creator* (1986), *Winter Term* is a heavily illustrated text adventure—though admittedly, the quality of the images varies wildly from location to location. There are many baffling references to characters who are presumably based on people known to the creators, but which fall flat due to the player's own lack of familiarity with the various in-jokes. However, the game also takes more general aim at the pop culture of the day, with visits to certain well-known high street retailers, jokes at the expense of British Rail, public libraries where overdue books have apparently become something of a sore point, and bored teenagers hanging around a filling station forecourt.

Winter Term suffers from its creators' rather 'interesting' choice of spelling and grammar, to say nothing of some decidedly eccentric choices of verb-noun commands which often need to be exactingly precise—usually at just the wrong moment. The game's map is similarly surreal (perhaps deliberately so), leading the player to some bizarre locations which in turn are adjacent to the least likely places. Puzzles include a jacket which inexplicably gives immunity from monsters (even when carried rather than actually worn), a painting which is somewhat bewilderingly regurgitated by a non-player character at a strangely convenient point, and a fair amount of object swapping and trading as the protagonist gradually edges closer to generating the necessary cash required to placate their disgruntled parent.

The game contains too many vast illogicalities to be considered a particularly effective text adventure, and much of the player's time is taken up trying to build a working awareness of the strangely-interlinked locations rather than wrestling with the threadbare variety of puzzles and decidedly basic parser that are on offer. It does, however, present a suitably grim portrayal of teenage life in the late 1980s for anyone nostalgic for the uninviting grey streets and miserable weather of their misspent youth. It may not offer up the kind of jolly Christmas fun for which most seasonal games have become better known, but for an irreverent take on the cold British winter there are few other titles which are quite so uncompromising in their portrayal of being young and broke in the UK of the eighties.

Quantum Sheep (2020)

Christmas and ladder-climbing sheep is not a combination that is regularly made in December (or at any other time of year, come to that). But with this colourful platform game, Quantum Sheep was to present a refreshingly unusual experience which brought back many happy memories of well-known eighties Spectrum arcade-style titles such as Elite's *Bomb Jack* (1986) and Firebird's *Bubble Bobble* (1987).

Quantum Sheep is a well-known figure on the retro gaming indie scene, having produced games for mobile platforms such as iOS and Android as well as desktop computers like the PC and Mac. An enigmatic figure, the Quantum Sheep has been involved in the games industry since the early 1990s, and they have been producing titles for mobile phones since the days of WAP gaming. Their games for the Spectrum include the entertaining railway-based platform action title *Last Train to Tranz-Central* (2020) and Victorian-era supernatural text adventure *The Séance* (2020), but the pleasingly surreal *Sheepy Xmas* came along at just the right time: at the end of a year that had seen the British public under repeated lockdown due to the COVID-19 coronavirus pandemic, and badly in need of cheering up as they approached the festive season.

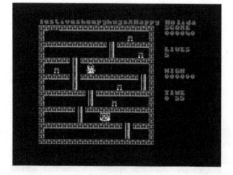

The gameplay is very straightforward. In the role of the Quantum Sheep themselves, the player is tasked with collecting presents to give to Santa in time for his Christmas Eve deliveries, though (inevitably) there are enemies on every screen scurrying around in an attempt to stop the hapless woolly quadruped in their tracks. Every now and again the sheep may be fortunate enough to spot a nice cup of tea, which results in an extra life. With 25 screens in all—split over five stages of five screens each—the game offers a leisurely challenge with plenty of knowing humour for the gaming veteran. In a nod to the games of yesteryear, both Kempston and Sinclair joysticks are supported, though redefinable keyboard play is also an option.

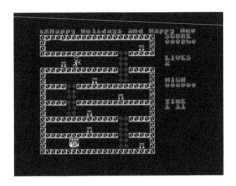

The 128K version of *Sheepy Xmas* includes some excellent festive music courtesy of 'Justinas', riffing on the melody of 'Jingle Bells' (though the 48K version still contains spot effects, meaning that the experience isn't entirely silent). Gameplay takes up around three-quarters of the screen, with the score, number of lives and remaining time limit displayed on the right-hand side.

Starting off with a generous allocation of five lives, the sheep must work their way through every stage sequentially. In a concession to the festive season, snow falls through the playing area, and a jovial Santa stands patiently at the top of every screen waiting for the parcels to be delivered into his hands. In the time-honoured tradition of *Pac-Man* and other arcade favourites, the sheep can also cross over from one edge of the screen to the other by passing through the outer border—something which becomes very useful if the sheep is to collect every gift while avoiding his enemies (including wind-up toys and so forth) who lack the ability to jump across the screen themselves. It is advisable not to underestimate the bad guys, however, as their seemingly-predictable movement patterns can sometimes change without notice—much to the sheep's detriment. Difficulty increases as the game's progress continues, and well-judged timing is particularly important if the sheep wants to collect every present in time.

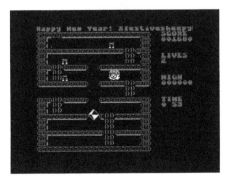

With plenty of good humour, and easy-to-learn gameplay that makes it especially well-suited to younger players, *Sheepy Xmas* presents some addictive festive action which perfectly encapsulated the best of eighties arcade action on the good old Speccy.

SANTA / X-MAZE

Artic Computing (1983)

Santa was an early compilation of mini-games from Artic Computing, a company perhaps better-known for its influential text adventure games as well as platform action titles such as *Bear Bovver* (1983) and *Mutant Monty* (1984). Based in Brandesburton, Artic was active from 1980 until 1986 and produced many games for early home computer systems such as the Sinclair ZX81. While the company was well-established by 1983, the Spectrum was still very much considered new technology at this point, and as such *Santa* was one of the first multi-game anthologies to appear on the machine.

Written in BASIC and exhibiting the limitations this might suggest, *Santa* is a pretty rudimentary take on the festive season—even by the standards of the Spectrum's early days. However, developers Jon Smith and Don Day certainly seemed determined to provide plenty of variety, and the game ambitiously contains six individual mini-games which can be selected after a simple rendition of 'Jingle Bells' has chirped out of their speaker.

All of the games are controlled using a combination of the 5, 6, 7 and 8 keys—still a decade and a half too early for any Steps jokes to be relevant. In 'Rudolph Goes Racing', everyone's favourite reindeer must manoeuvre up and down to avoid collision with trees in a wintry North Pole forest; too many bumps and the race is over. 'Burst the Balloons' sees Santa darting left and right in an attempt to intercept vertically-scrolling balloons as they rise up the screen. With every balloon he misses, Jolly Old St Nick moves one step closer to the bottom of the screen, making it progressively more difficult to catch the helium-filled targets. '12 Days of Xmas' sees the screen filled with items from the traditional yuletide song, and the player is tasked with collecting them in order (first a partridge in a pear tree, then two turtle doves, etc.) while avoiding the others until their time has come.

With 'Peek in the Pudding', the player is again invited to take up the role of Santa, who must dig his way through a gigantic Christmas pudding in search of hidden gold coins. Accidentally find a worm instead, however, and it's game over. In 'Stop the Snowflakes', Santa is controlling a beam which must be swept left and right in an attempt to catch falling snowflakes as they scroll vertically down the screen, in a manner similar to a frosty version of *Missile Command*. A counter keeps track of how many snowflakes are caught and how many are missed, offering an overall rating at the end of the turn. 'Stack the Stocking' gives poor Santa yet another task, in that he must catch vertically falling presents and deliver them into a giant Christmas stocking. His hit/miss ratio is tallied as the action unfolds.

On the B-side of the game cassette was a separate seventh feature: *X-Maze*. This was a festively-themed maze game programmed by Jon Smith and also written in BASIC. With a variable difficulty level ranging from 1 (easy) to 9 (difficult), Santa must escape from a maze while keeping his strength level up and his number of bruises—caused by collisions—down as much as possible. There are doorways to explore and presents to collect, but the hapless Father Christmas must also watch out for rampaging nasties inhabiting the maze—often in the least expected of places.

Originally released at a mid-range £5.95 price point, *Santa* was met with general indifference from the trade press at the time. Reviewers accepted that the game's simple action was obviously aimed at younger players, but lamented the brevity of the mini-games. While the graphics are uniformly primitive, *Santa* was still noteworthy for its sheer aspiration in attempting to present a truly varied gaming experience at such a formative point in the life of the Spectrum.

CONTESTANT TC   ATTEMPT 1

WINTER GAMES

US Gold/Epyx (1986)

No fewer than three Winter Olympic Games took place throughout the eighties—Lake Placid in 1980, Sarajevo in 1984, and Calgary in 1988—and these famous international multi-sport events were to influence many computer games during the course of the decade. One of the best and most fondly remembered on the Spectrum was *Winter Games*, a hotly-anticipated release from Epyx and US Gold which certainly didn't disappoint when it hit the market back in 1986.

Available in both 48K and 128K formats (the latter featuring some excellent musical accompaniment), *Winter Games* presented players of the time with a full roster of challenges which reflected the numerous different disciplines of the Olympiad. Gamers were given the option of competing in all of the events sequentially; taking part in a particular selection; or simply practising one or more events to hone their skills. Up to four players could compete, the roster consisting of any combination of human and computer-controlled characters. In true Olympic fashion, the race was then well and truly on to compete for gold, silver and bronze medals, depending on the players' performance in any given category.

The game certainly looked the part with its chilly ambience, and it wastes no time in getting straight on with the events—and a memorable line-up it proves to be. The action is split over two separate days (and, as luck would have it, two different sides of the game cassette). The first day includes hot dog aerials, where the player skis off a short ledge and has a brief period of time to demonstrate as many mid-air stunts as possible. The trick here is

35

to kick, dive and somersault as much as possible while still giving the character just enough time to land in one piece. Speed skating involves that halcyon skill of computer sports games, namely waggling the joystick left and right as quickly as you can, in order to propel the player forward as fast as possible. A split-screen ice rink divides the action between either two human players, or the player and a computer-controlled character. Rounding off the first day of events is the ski jump. This time the player has a far longer slope to initiate their jump, and their performance is rated based on a combination of how far they travel along with their successful landing. Fail to correct their posture and stance, and the character is more likely than not to hit the ground rather too rapidly—and with the possible inclusion of a few broken bones into the bargain.

Day two involves figure skating, where the player is tasked with packing a full array of different manoeuvres into a performance lasting no more than a minute. They must squeeze in as many moves as possible while avoiding stumbles or indeed falling over, as any graceless mistakes will result in points being deducted from their routine's overall score. Free skating presented a very similar event, the difference being that the player now has

a two-minute limit on their performance and must make more attempts to fit the various different available movements into their routine (while similarly avoiding any unfortunate tumbles along the way). The biathlon is a gruelling combination of skiing and target shooting, alternating between the two skills at key points. The left/right joystick waggle was once again in evidence as the player must battle to maintain a uniform speed as they scroll past some eye-catching, mountainous scenery. At various points along the course, a rifle range is presented, and the player must take careful aim in order to hit each target; failing to shoot accurately will lead to penalty points being accrued against their total score. Finally, there is the bobsled event. Here, the screen is split between an aerial map of the course and a third-person view of the bobsled as it manoeuvres along the trench and its various bends. The player must navigate the track as quickly as possible whilst anticipating every turn; steering too sharply into the bend, or not steering quickly enough, may lead to the bobsled overturning—and yet another embarrassing visit to the local hospital's Accident and Emergency department.

Winter Games was a hugely popular title for US Gold, and was reissued numerous times on different labels as well as becoming a regular fixture on many compilation packs in subsequent years. The game performed well with the critics too, as the trade press reacted very favourably to its brisk pace, diverse range of events and appealing graphics. Some reviewers also commended the way in which the action varied masterfully between battling the clock, alternating through different manoeuvres or moves, and relying on fast reflexes. Due to its convenient ability to load all of the different events in a single go, rather than having to flip the tape and play the events in two separate sessions, the 128K version also came in for praise.

With its well-judged variety of sporting activities, relying on manifold gameplay types (and a welcome departure from the perpetual joystick-mashing of other sports titles such as Imagine's *Hyper Sports* or Ocean's infamous *Daley Thompson's Decathlon*), *Winter Games* quickly established itself as a firm favourite amongst armchair sports fans on the Spectrum, and it led to numerous other competitive events games from the US Gold stable appearing on the Spectrum including *Summer Games* (1988) and *California Games* (1988). In its highly-polished presentation of winter sporting events, however, it was it was rarely to be equalled as an Olympic simulator—much less bettered.

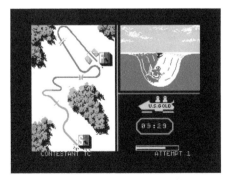

ALL PRESENT AND CORRECT

Bob Smith (2009)

Wouldn't Christmas be a lot easier on Santa and his elves if all of our festive gifts simply jogged into delivery bags under their own steam? That is the premise of Bob Smith's innovative puzzle game *All Present and Correct*, which invites the player to aid in the process of preparing for the Christmas rush by ensuring that all of the presents make it safely into Santa's toy sacks rather than disappearing into oblivion through any of the inconveniently-placed holes which pepper the playing area. As if that wasn't troublesome enough, marauding hammers swing around with the intention of smashing up the gifts in they should unwittingly drift into their path.

The action of *All Present and Correct* is heavily influenced by Sonic Team's 1999 puzzler *ChuChu Rocket!* (published by Sega) which appeared on the Dreamcast and Game Boy Advance before later making the jump to Android and iOS mobile devices. In the same manner as that earlier game, the player is tasked with strategically placing directional arrows which guide the characters along a particular vector. Whereas *ChuChu Rocket!* involved protecting hapless mice from falling into the clutches of predatory cats, however, *All Present and Correct* was to see players corralling little parcels with legs and leading them towards the safety of a delivery sack before they can be whacked by a passing hammer or fall down a hole in the playing area like a misplaced pool ball.

With short but functional musical ditties and plenty of cute sprites wandering around the playing area like an accident just waiting to happen, *All Present and Correct* certainly had plenty of presentational appeal, but it is the game's level of addictiveness which will incline gamers to keep coming back for more. With such a deceptively simple premise and an impeccably-considered difficulty level, the game starts off with a few straightforward levels and then gradually but unforgivingly ratchets up the trickiness. Players will find much to enjoy in trying to fathom the likely direction of the hapless Christmas packages as they shuffle around—their ultimate safety (or otherwise) being dependent on the user's foresight.

With a total of forty levels, and even the inclusion of a level editor so that players can concoct their own fiendish convolutions for others to try out, the game certainly packs in plenty of playability to maintain interest. As the levels progress, players will find themselves faced with ever more complex scenarios—herding more and more parcels into multiple delivery bags with only a frugal selection of directional arrows (shown in a column along the right-hand side of the screen) available to aid their efforts.

Bob Smith is a well-known figure in the world of retro gaming, his website *Bob's Stuff* being home to numerous inventive latter-day Spectrum titles. His work has included the ingenious dominoes-meets-*Tetris* mash-up *Dominetris* (2005), appealing assembly line-based platformer *Factory Daze* (2009), and the visually-arresting isometric puzzle game $X=Y=Z$ (2014), amongst many others—including numerous ambitious titles and 'demakes' for the Sinclair ZX81. While he has become particularly recognised for his work in the puzzle game genre, the festively-themed *All Present and Correct* stands out as an especially fun diversion for the long winter nights—and it certainly makes the most of the Spectrum's technical resources to present a refined product which draws players in with its initial simplicity, but soon has them hooked on its brain-meltingly intricate dynamics.

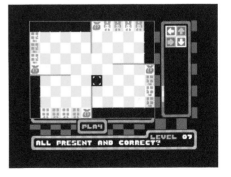

THE WOODS OF WINTER

CRL Group (1984)

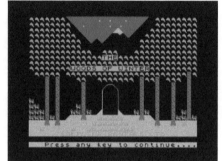

The text adventures of the Spectrum have taken users on some memorable excursions through extreme environments over the years, but rarely was navigating through hostile terrain the actual subject of the game. Not so for *The Woods of Winter*, a title which presented a simple but effective premise: to get away from the bitter cold of the harsh elements and reach the warmth of a nearby castle.

The game's classy packaging artwork by Phil Gascoine suggests a mediaeval fantasy setting common to much interactive fiction of the time, but in reality the game presented a rather more abstract playing experience than might be expected from the swords-and-sorcery ambiance that the cover implies. There is no elaborate scenario to set the scene: the player is simply thrust straight in to the action, starting the game on a moss-covered spiral staircase, and must devise a way of surviving the cold long enough to travel through the forbidding woods to the safety of the fortress beyond.

Although it does not feature location illustrations per sé, *The Woods of Winter* was highly unusual for the time in that the top two-thirds of the screen displayed a map of the surrounding area which takes shape as the player travels around, making the game considerably easier to navigate. The trade-off from this innovation was that the response time from each command was much lengthier than most other text adventures of the

40

period, with the game taking several seconds to process textual input before displaying the results.

The game's creator, Andrew Patrick, does a good job of building a sense of chilly foreboding around the proceedings—not an easy task given the scant location descriptions—and while the parser is comparatively basic it is nonetheless serviceable enough. There are a few spelling anomalies scattered around the game ('chisil' in place of 'chisel', for instance), but none which are likely to spoil the player's enjoyment by over-complicating matters. In spite of the clear-cut concept, the game contains some effective and well-thought-out puzzles and should provide even the adventuring novice with a pleasant challenge to solve.

The Woods of Winter was a quirky and original game which presented players with a good mix of the traditional and the inventive. Though the speed of the responses can slow the action to a crawl at times, the game has plenty of charm and even a sense of humour with some nicely-pitched in-jokes to be found here and there. (In particular, watch out for a clever allusion to Ocean Software's much-played 1984 platform game *Hunchback*.)

CRL (originally Computer Rentals Limited) was an instantly-recognisable software label in the eighties, and became especially well-known for their excellent range of text adventures including the sublime Delta 4 games as well as many other superb interactive fiction titles such as the work of St Bride's School and the controversial Rod Pike literary horror adaptations, which famously carried British Board of Film Classification ratings due to their graphic content. *The Woods of Winter* may not have been the most memorable interactive fiction title that the company released amongst their prolific commercial output, nor was it their most critically successful. However, for a bit of atmospheric entertainment it was a welcome diversion; simply escaping the cold was a breath of fresh air compared to the high-stakes challenges of so many other adventure games.

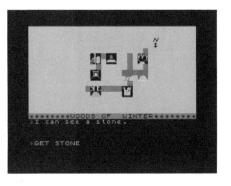

RUPERT AND THE ICE CASTLE

Bug-Byte Software/War on Want (1986)

For generations of British children, Christmas just wouldn't be Christmas without a *Rupert the Bear* annual tucked under their tree. The titular ursine resident of the woodland village of Nutwood has been entertaining children in the *Daily Express* newspaper since November 1920, and his creator Mary Tourtel could scarcely have imagined the vast appeal that the character would have. Later popularised by writer and artist Alfred Bestall between 1935 and 1974, Rupert became so beloved of young people throughout the UK that annuals bearing his name have been sold every year since 1936—and famously, this included right throughout World War II when Britain was hit by a paper shortage during the conflict. The famous bear and his friends have continued to gain new fans ever since, and the popularity of the franchise shows no sign of diminishing even now, more than a century after the character first appeared.

With his firmly-established status as a British pop culture icon (and who could forget Paul McCartney's 1984 song with the frog chorus, 'We All Stand Together', which reached number three in the UK singles charts?), It was only a matter of time before Rupert made the jump into the world of home computing, and this eventually came in 1985 with Quicksilva's platform game *Rupert and the Toymaker's Party*, which divided the critics of the time. This colourful title did, however, nicely capture the fantasy settings and charming sense of whimsy which had long characterised the newspaper comic strip, so it came as no surprise that the sanguine, scarf-wearing little bear would make a rather more seasonal appearance the following year in the form of *Rupert and the Ice Castle*.

Building on the platform action dynamics of its predecessor with an even more finely-honed presentation, *Rupert and the Ice Castle* was produced by Bug-Byte Software and made its first commercial appearance on the widely-publicised game compilation pack *WOW Games*: a release which had been made possible by the involvement of anti-poverty charity War on Want. Challenging social injustice and inequality since 1951, War on Want has been involved in campaigns to raise public awareness of the issues caused by poverty for decades, so the organisation's move into the increasingly popular world of computer gaming was a logical step—not only did it raise proceeds towards the charity's causes, but the title's release also heightened awareness of their work amongst the public. The *WOW Games* compilation was excellent value for money, including fourteen titles ranging from chess through to maze exploration games.

As its title suggests, *Rupert and the Ice Castle* sees our hero braving the interior of a wintry fortress in which Jenny Frost (mischievous sister of the rather more famous Jack Frost) has kidnapped several of his friends from the comic strip, including Bill Badger, Algy Pug and others. Thankfully Rupert is on hand with a supply of 'ice pills', which have the power to defrost his acquaintances long enough for them to find their way home to Nutwood. All he has to do is manoeuvre his way through each level, climbing the various platforms while avoiding the numerous hazards which get in his way. These include icy puddles which cause him to slip, skates which move back and forth across the playing area, and other dangers such as bouncing eggs and jack-in-the-boxes which can move from level to level.

Rupert the Bear is Copyright © Classic Media Distribution Ltd./Express Newspapers

The game makes good use of the icy environment, not least in the way that the white and blue palette contrasts effectively with Rupert's famous red and yellow clothing. The graphics are nicely detailed, even in spite of the Spectrum's notorious colour clash, and all of the familiar characters are immediately recognisable. Gameplay is uncomplicated enough for younger players to get involved in the action right away, but with sixteen different screens to master (each of them featuring a rhyming couplet, just like the text which accompanies the illustrations in Rupert's *Daily Express* appearances) there is a gradually increasing level of difficulty which means that the various stages will require patience and skill to complete. Icicles fall from the ceiling, seemingly-friendly snowmen are not what they seem, and other perils will present themselves as the game progresses. In later levels, Rupert must collect warm clothing to counteract the plunging temperatures, and if he runs out of ice pills (their number diminishes every time he comes in contact with an antagonist) then he must abandon his rescue efforts and the game is over. See things through to the end, however, and the player is rewarded with a conclusion sequence featuring Rupert and the castle's rightful owner.

Reviewers of the time praised the game's large, colourful characters, its general gloss and level of playability, but expressed disappointment in the lack of musical accompaniment and weak range of sound effects. The relative ease of completion was excused by the fact that the title is aimed primarily at children, while others noted the sheer value for money being offered by the fact that a brand new game was being included with so many other (re-released) titles as part of the charity compilation. This did, admittedly, cause some to note the slightly unusual fact that a winter-themed title was appearing for the first time in the height of summer, but a bear is not just for Christmas and—for his many fans—Rupert's icy antics proved to be just as entertaining when December arrived.

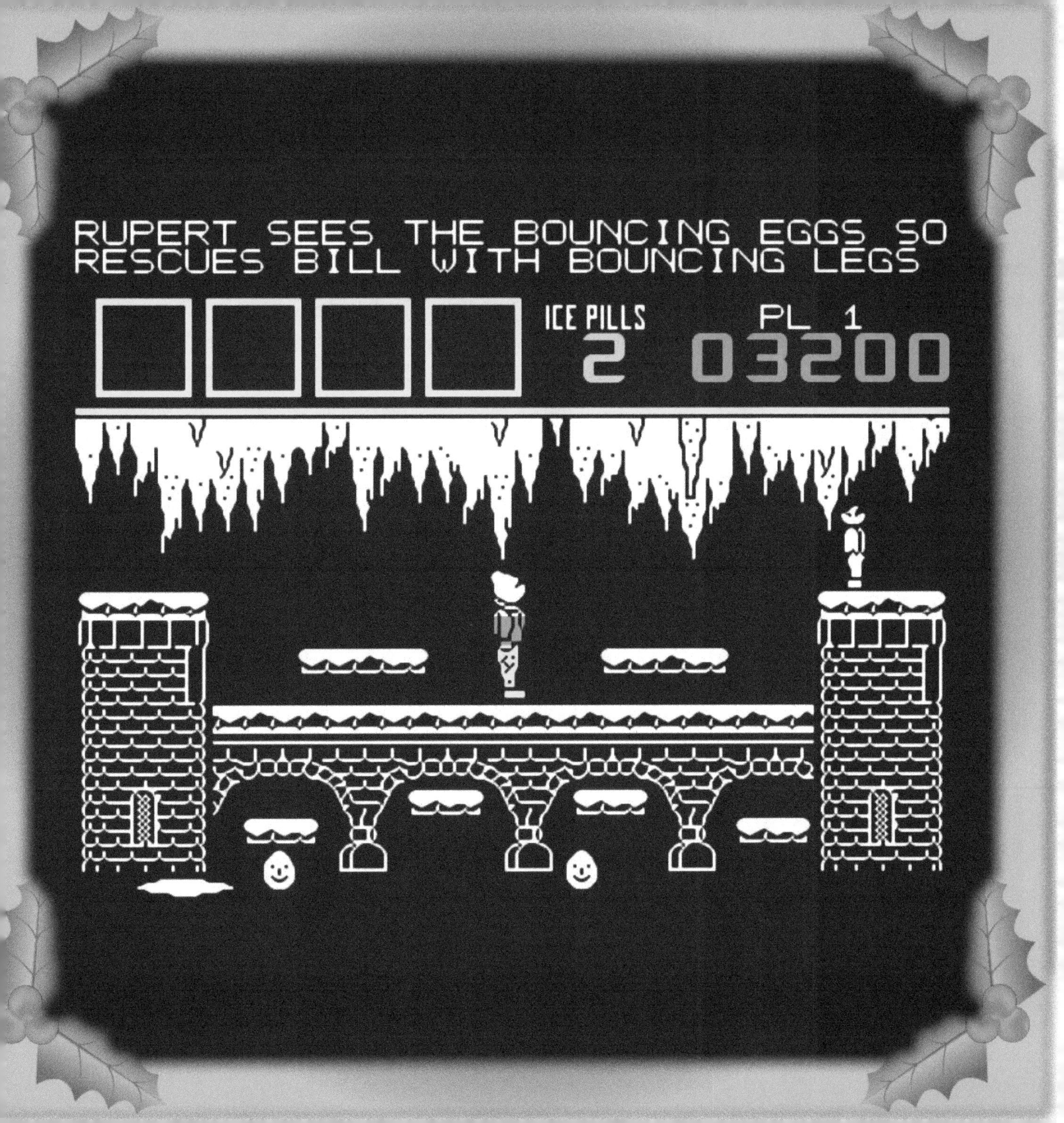
RUPERT SEES THE BOUNCING EGGS SO
RESCUES BILL WITH BOUNCING LEGS
ICE PILLS
2
PL 1
03200

ROBOT SANTA

Simon D. Lee (2014)

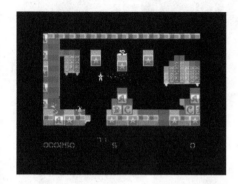

Robot Santa is something of a modern mystery amongst Christmas games on the Spectrum. Emerging onto the retro gaming scene in 2014, this impressive platform title was created by Simon D. Lee using *The Arcade Game Designer* and immediately catches the player's attention with its detailed and brightly-coloured playing area. The reason for its enigmatic reputation, however, comes from the fact that the game doesn't seem to have been completely finished, and its curtailed development has inevitably led to some head-scratching as to what the story is actually about.

With no title screen or opening sequence, or indeed even instructions, part of the fun of *Robot Santa* is trying to work out what's going on as you play. In the bottom quarter of the screen there are counters displaying the player's high score, number of lives and an energy gauge, but it's quite obvious from the way these figures are strategically situated that there was supposed to be a graphic surrounding them to indicate what each of them are—an illustration that was ultimately never added.

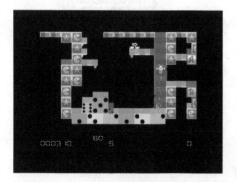

Get beyond the inevitable rough edges that come with an unfinished game, however, and *Robot Santa* is an admirable achievement for a Spectrum title. While discerning the details of the plot is rather tricky, it seems that the player controls a robotic version of Santa (which appears to look a little bit like a cross between a jack-in-the-box and a decorative nutcracker) tasked with collecting presents from his workshop in the North Pole. Or alternatively, perhaps the character is facing the challenge of collecting parts of a robot Santa which must be assembled in time for the Christmas Eve deliveries to take place. It's likely that we'll never know for sure. What is more certain, however, is that the game involves manoeuvring around the area by jumping from platform to platform, avoiding errant antagonists which flit back and forth while trying to collect items (which, in the grand tradition of the genre, are usually placed in the least accessible places imaginable). Electric fans on the ground can propel our hero high into the air, and occasionally a power vortex will be encountered which has the ability to replenish the player's energy level.

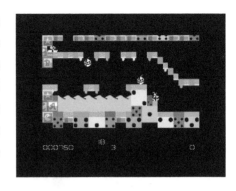

The game's bright and cheerful playing area is packed with festive trimmings and childhood gaming favourites such as dice and alphabet building blocks, and recalls the visual style of Millennium Software's legendary Commodore Amiga platformer *James Pond 2: Codename Robocod* (1991). There is no music to accompany the action—just a few nondescript spot effects—which does let the side down a bit. Similarly, the game would have benefited from a larger sprite for the main character; even with the 3D effect that is applied to the various platforms, the central figure tends to get lost against the background (and its own lack of colour can make it difficult to see at the best of times). However, the animations are smooth and the collision detection is relatively merciful, so gameplay is not too adversely affected by the illusion that the protagonist is more or less continually swamped by their own surroundings.

Robot Santa has all the hallmarks of a latter-day platform game classic on the Spectrum, and it's a great pity that it was never completed—indeed, it is clear from the main playing experience that it must surely have been so close to being finished that only aspects such as a loading screen, options menu and background illustrations are obvious omissions. Aside from these loose ends, the game is as visually appealing as any of the best evocations of Santa's North Pole HQ and provides an excellent example of what the Spectrum's hardware can do when in the right hands.

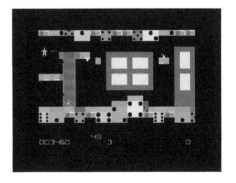

FROST BYTE

Mikro-Gen (1986)

Almost certainly the most tenuous inclusion in this book, I am the first to admit that *Frost Byte* is not exactly a festive classic: playing out in the ice caverns of an alien ice world, it isn't by any means the epitome of conventional wintry settings. (Nor indeed does it bear any resemblance to Activision's similarly-named 1983 ice floe-hopping classic *Frostbite* for the Atari 2600, where igloo-building was the order of the day.) Look beyond the outlandish scenario, however, and the game's off-kilter charm makes it a worthwhile diversion for players who are looking for something a little bit different from their virtual environments.

Mikro-Gen was an instantly-recognisable developer in the era of the 8-bit home computer, especially well-known for introducing the hapless family man Wally Week and his range of graphic adventures which included *Automania* (1984), *Pyjamarama* (1984), *Herbert's Dummy Run* (1985), *Three Weeks in Paradise* (1986) and—most famously—*Everyone's a Wally* (1985). The company produced many titles in its time, including management simulators, role-playing games and the highly ambitious graphic adventure *Shadow of the Unicorn* (1985). *Frost Byte* was a characteristically offbeat title for Mikro-Gen, introducing many cross-genre gameplay elements to create a distinctive (if at times slightly baffling) experience.

The game is set on the planet Cosmica and stars a creature named Hickey who belongs to a race called Kreezers. Hickey has managed to escape captivity, and now faces an uphill struggle to free his fellow Kreezers from the clutches of the fearsome monsters who have taken over the planet's ice caves. There is only one problem: Hickey has the form of a humble slinky—a little metal spring which turns over from end to end (incidentally, a popular Christmas gift of yesteryear)—and thus will require a bit of extra help when it comes to liberating his compatriots. This comes in the form of ammunition which can be fired at enemies, and a range of different energy sweets which, when ingested, offers him different abilities such as being able to move faster, jump higher or fall further. Time is against him, however, for if the 'twang-o-meter' runs out then it will be too late for his captured friends and they will be devoured by the marauding monsters.

With a plot as bizarre as this, the player deserves points just for getting started. But don't be deceived: in spite of the scene-setting convolutions, the game plays well and is full of rewarding surprises. Though it takes a while to get into the habit of controlling a sentient slinky, the controls are strangely intuitive and the well laid-out display panel at the bottom of the screen clearly displays the item Hickey is holding, the number of fellow Kreezers still to be rescued, and the amount of lives he has remaining.

Featuring large, chunky sprites and impressively fluid motion of animation, *Frost Byte* always looks great, and with a large map spread over five levels—each filled with increasingly absurd enemies—a sense of progression is conveyed by the gradually changing environment as Hickey moves from the frozen depths of the ice caverns towards the subtropical climate above. (Players catch a glimpse of the planet's surface in the final stage.)

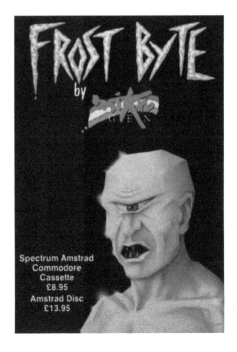

Reviewers of the eighties were largely approving of the game's merits, drawing particular attention to its astute puzzle-solving elements and the way that it cleverly blended visual aspects of other classic games such as *Underwurlde* (1984) and *Nodes of Yesod* (1985). It may not be dripping with yuletide atmosphere, admittedly, but it still contains plenty of frosty appeal nonetheless. After all, we can't be certain that they don't celebrate Christmas on alien worlds like Cosmica... can we?

XMAS-OID

Stonechat Productions (2020)

Game designer Dave Hughes is no stranger to a Christmas theme—many of his titles have taken the festive season as their focus, and have been released through his software company Snapchat Productions which has been popularising brand new software for the Sinclair Spectrum even now, almost four decades after the machine was first released. First appearing on *WOOT! Tape Magazine*'s issue four, the game was a characteristically inventive blend of the traditional and the offbeat.

Xmas-oid features as its central character an atom of hydrogen, whose preparations for the Christmas holidays (let's just roll with it) are disrupted when its home is invaded by strange creatures. In order to defeat them, the atom must manoeuvre from platform to platform collecting Christmas crackers, then escape to the next level via a flashing exit square. So far, so *Manic Miner*... or so it may seem at face value. For while the game may contain similar types of enemies familiar to many vintage platformers—not least metal spikes which fall and rise from the floor and require perfect timing to avoid—the action is actually quite different.

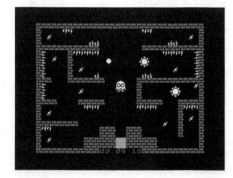

As the player quickly realises, the game's atomic protagonist doesn't simply jump from one ledge to another in the familiar style of Miner Willy and his ilk. Instead, the atom is rotated left and right using the 'O' and 'P' keys, while it is propelled forward by use of the 'Z' key. Thus in one fell swoop the game leaves *Chuckie Egg* territory and becomes something much closer to Firebird Software's infamously frustrating classic *Thrust* (1986), complete with a similar recreation of momentum and ricochet dynamics.

Xmas-oid can probably be most appropriately described as exasperating in the best possible way: the concept behind the atom's movement is very simple to learn in principle, but strangely disorienting when it comes to moving around while averting collision with enemies and lethal obstacles. Similarly, colliding with the walls at speed will cause the atom to rebound, potentially striking something as it does so. Thankfully the collision detection is as refined as it possibly could be, meaning that close scrapes do not necessarily lead to the sudden death of the player's character.

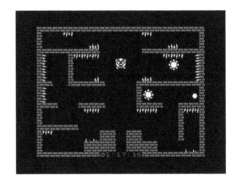

There is no limit on the number of lives the player has to complete the game, though a timer keeps track of the amount of time it takes for them to safely navigate the playing area while collecting all of the crackers. This may take longer than expected, as a number of the traps and obstacles will require split-second timing if the atom is to avoid them and pass by unscathed. Adding another element of challenge is the fact that once the final cracker has been picked up, one of the enemies immediately races to take up residence within the exit portal. If the player doesn't beat them to it, there will be no way of completing the level. (No pressure there, then!)

With some excellently jaunty music by Sergio Vaquer Montes and graphics that will make any Spectrum gamer nostalgic for the machine's glory days, *Xmas-oid* is certainly a slick production—as you would expect from its creator—and really the only disappointment is that it finishes so abruptly. Consisting of only one level, it won't take too long for most players to complete, though there is certainly a temptation to replay it a few times just to see if the completion time can be driven down. (Choosing different paths through the screen, and timing the approach around certain obstacles, can shave off a few vital seconds here and there.) While its brevity means it is unlikely that the game will become a modern Christmas classic, there is certainly plenty of slightly maddening fun to be had... provided you don't mind turning the air blue as you lose your hundredth life thanks to a slightly misjudged turn at the worst possible moment.

GARFIELD: WINTER'S TAIL

The Edge (1990)

Garfield was one of the most ubiquitous characters of the 1980s: not only had the Paws, Inc. cartoon strips been enduringly popular since artist Jim Davis first conceived the character in 1976 (and indeed remain so today), but the sarcastic marmalade-hued kitty was already in the process of making the jump into the world of TV animation and would eventually be awarded a Guinness World Record for being the world's most widely-syndicated comic strip in 2002; a remarkable achievement. It was difficult to find a car in the eighties that didn't have a cuddly Garfield stuck to the inside of its windows or dangling from the rear-view mirror, so with the franchise's merchandise enjoying such a sky-high profile across the world it seemed inevitable that a leap into the home computer market would be imminent.

The Edge enjoyed great success on the Spectrum with titles such as isometric exploration games *Fairlight* (1985) and *Inside Outing* (1988), platform action game *Brian Bloodaxe* (1985) and arcade conversion *Shao-Lin's Road* (1986), but the company was to be especially fondly remembered for its comic strip adaptations *Snoopy* (1990) and *Garfield: Big Fat Hairy Deal* (1988). Both of these games employed large, detailed sprites within the framework of an arcade adventure format, visiting familiar characters and environments from the original comics with more than enough fidelity to impress reviewers and delight fans.

Given the critical success of the original, there were high expectations for *Garfield: Winter's Tail* (sometimes subtitled 'A Midsupper Night's Dream'), which was to take a very different approach to its action. The scenario revolves around Garfield, in a deep sleep in the kitchen of his home, dreaming of an amazing quest to the Alps. (The fact that his bed is situated next to a chilly refrigerator may just be influencing his subconscious mind.) This leads to a series of adventures starting with a vertically-scrolling ski race to the bottom of a mountain (accompanied by Odie, his canine companion and sometime annoyance) where he must constantly veer and jump around various obstacles while keeping his strength up by collecting plates of lasagne being offered by his owner, the hapless Jon Arbuckle.

Reach the base of the mountain in one piece, and Garfield has the chance of tucking into a king's ransom-worth of his favourite pasta dish at an Italian lasagne kitchen, where a bit of right-and-left joystick waggling will see the famously hungry feline stuffed to bursting point. Once he has recovered from his scoffing session, he can head off to a chocolate factory just over the Alps in Switzerland in search of a legendary chicken that lays chocolate eggs. To achieve this, he must deliver liquid chocolate from a system of pipes to the chickens within the factory—only by a process of elimination can he determine where the mythical chicken is located, but until then he'll need to keep up his strength by collecting food wherever he can find it... and before the affable-but-dim Odie can eat it first.

The game concludes with a trek through a maze atop a frozen lake as Garfield straps on his ice skates and pursues the chocolate egg-laying chicken by following its tracks. He must exercise great care, lest he lose control on the slippery surface and collide with the hazards that are scattered around the area. The maze is fairly capacious, however—and complete with the ominous letters 'H-E-L-P' at its centre—suggesting that Garfield will need all of his wits about him if he is to successfully navigate

Garfield is Copyright © Paws, Inc./Viacom

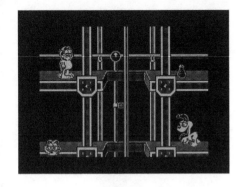

his way to the other side of the lake and meet the chicken that can make his chocolate egg-themed fantasy complete.

Garfield: Winter's Tail met with a lukewarm response from the trade press reviewers of the time, who praised the detailed graphics which perfectly recreated Jim Davis's lovable characters but dismissed the gameplay as slow and repetitive. A common complaint was that although the four minigames seemed superficially different, the action still felt lacking in variety, with some aspects (such as the downhill skiing section) being too easy to complete while others (the chocolate factory, for instance) were unduly fiddly and plodding. The curious decision not to include the player's score on-screen also added to the feeling of interchangeability.

The lack of colour, which was an unfortunate limitation of the Spectrum's technical abilities, didn't help matters as it gave the various wintry playing areas a rather washed-out, homogenous appearance that did a disservice to the larger-than-life figures who were populating it. However, the game did benefit from having a selectable starting level, meaning that if players became tired of the action on any particular stage of the game they had the option of skipping it altogether and jumping to the next stage.

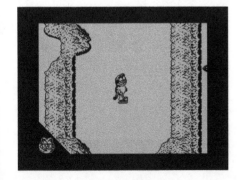

While the snowy escapades it presents are sometimes head-scratchingly eccentric, perhaps the biggest drawback of *Garfield: Winter's Tail* is its strange lack of wintry atmosphere. The backgrounds just seem too generic. Even with its strangely disjointed narrative, there is no denying the game's ambition, but it never quite manages to shake a sense of formulaic banality. Given the success of its predecessor, which was widely praised for bringing the locations of the much-loved cartoon strip to life, maybe pulling Garfield out of his familiar Indiana-based surroundings had compromised some of his unique charm in the process. While the game will remain of interest to Garfield aficionados, for many the lasting impression will be one of wasted opportunity.

THE TWELVE DAYS OF CHRISTMAS

Zenobi Software (1994)

One of the best-loved traditional English Christmas carols (though actually believed to be French in origin), 'The Twelve Days of Christmas' has been a staple of British winter festivities since at least 1780 and over the years has been hugely influential in popular culture. This folk song has been endlessly performed and parodied, not least the belting out of the 'Five Golden Rings' verse which has been famously prolonged since the time of Frederic Austin's musical arrangement which appeared in 1909. With many people learning the song in their schooldays it holds a special place in the hearts of many, though in recent years there has been increasing scepticism over how many people have a true love who would actually want to receive quite such a grandiose number of wild birds (and other similarly bizarre phenomena) as a yuletide gift.

On the face of it, the song's cumulative narrative of one gift after another suggests the perfect scenario for a home computer title, though it is perhaps most suggestive of the kind of item-collection action that was popularised by so many platform-based action adventure games. Instead, interactive fiction creator Diane Rice decided to develop the concept into a text adventure game—a particularly good one, as it happens—which challenges the player to collect all twelve of the gifts for their (somewhat demanding) true love in order to ensure a happy Christmas for all.

With text boldly displayed in the traditional festive colours of red and green for some immediate Christmas atmosphere, the game gets right into the thick of the action from the get-go, displaying a full list of the gifts from each of the twelve days and then tasking the player to start tracking them down. Rice was perhaps best recognised for her fantasy text adventures written for the Spectrum, *A Serpentine Tale* (1993) and *The Black Tower* (1993), and while certainly there are a few stylistic trappings of these medievalist tropes to be found in *The Twelve Days of Christmas* they certainly don't dominate proceedings. Quite the contrary, in fact—the game offers an entertaining and decidedly unique playing experience which alternates very effectively between the everyday and the dreamlike.

As the player moves from one in-game environment to another, part of the enjoyment of exploring the locations is trying to anticipate what kind of curve-ball the designer has chosen to throw at the player—many of the twelve gifts are not at all what they appear to be, and often it is just as intricate a task to identify the item that is needed as it is to actually collect it for delivery to the protagonist's true love. The game was designed with the aid of Gilsoft's famous text adventure creator *The Quill*, and given the number of locations and items required to complete it the action is split over three separate parts; access to the latter two is gained by inputting a password which is given to the player on finishing the previous section.

The parser is perfectly functional and, while no especially complex commands are necessary to see the game through, there are plenty of clever puzzles to tax the grey matter of all but the most seasoned text adventurer. Sometimes action is required within a limited number of moves—for instance, at one point the main character is bitten by a poisonous snake and has only a short period to discover a cure before the venom in their system proves fatal. There is a lot of playability in all three parts of the game, with whimsical fairytale magic rubbing shoulders quite amiably with science fiction conventions and occasionally more mundane solutions to the problems that are presented for the player to tackle. There is also a fair bit of tongue-in-cheek humour to enjoy, though it should be noted that—while the game has a fairly relaxed level of difficulty—it is not devoid of fatal situations which can stop progress in its tracks. Similarly, effective mapping is essential in several places if the player seeks to avoid becoming hopelessly lost and forced to restore their position from earlier in the game.

Perhaps inspired by that great work of festive drama, *The Twelfth Night*, all three of the game's parts have Shakespearean-themed titles such as *The Course of True Love*, *Love's Labours* and *All's Well...* Each one will require time, skill and patience to complete, but the constant alternation of styles and playing environments always obviates any chance of the action ever becoming stale or repetitive. And while variety may be the order of the day, the game does manage to maintain an impressive line in festive jollity throughout.

The Twelve Days of Christmas was published by Zenobi Software, one of the most enduring success stories of the Spectrum gaming world. Specialising in text adventure games, this independent software house—based in Rochdale—was established by its owner John Wilson in 1986 and continued to sell its titles via mail order until 1997, long after the machine's golden age was over. The company continued to operate in various forms until 2013, and testament to the popularity of its titles and size of its catalogue—which included games such as *An Everyday Tale of a Seeker of Gold* (1986), *Bulbo and the Lizard King* (1987) and *Agatha's Folly* (1989)—the Zenobi brand endured in one form or another until Wilson's death in 2021.

While it may not have been Zenobi's most high-profile title, *The Twelve Days of Christmas* is an impressive and entertaining slice of interactive fiction which contains enough yuletide idiosyncrasy to bring a smile to the face of all but the most Scrooge-like of players.

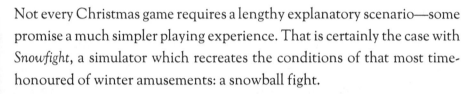

SNOWFIGHT

Firesoftware (2002)

Not every Christmas game requires a lengthy explanatory scenario—some promise a much simpler playing experience. That is certainly the case with *Snowfight*, a simulator which recreates the conditions of that most time-honoured of winter amusements: a snowball fight.

Created by Estonia's Alexei Teplyakov, the game has a very straightforward concept. The player must gather loose snow into a ball, throw it at their opponent, and attempt to hit them with it more often than they end up being hit themselves. There is a third-person perspective to proceedings, with the two competitors staring at each other across a snowy expanse. Not the most convoluted principle by any means, but sometimes the easiest ideas to learn can be amongst the most entertaining in practice.

There is a choice between either two human players taking part, or competing directly against the computer. In spite of the sparseness of the central action, the game is surprisingly customisable with options such as redefinable controls, a changeable time of day for the action to take place, and the total number of hits required to win the game. Then it is simply a case of making a snowball, choosing a direction to throw it in, and attempting to dodge any incoming fire from your rival.

Snowfight harks back to the earliest days of Spectrum gaming, both in its graphical presentation and its gameplay, but arguably its origins go even further back to 1970s arcade games such as Taito's *Gunfight* (1975) and Midway's *Boot Hill* (1977). For a quick blast, it's a fun enough diversion.

CHRISTMAS CRACKER SIMULATOR

Textvoyage (2018)

The humble Christmas cracker has been gracing dinner tables in Britain, Ireland, Canada, New Zealand, Australia, South Africa and many other countries for almost two centuries. Invented by confectioner Tom Smith of London in 1847, who popularised the idea of a bon-bon sweet with a love message added to the wrapper, the concept soon caught the public imagination thanks to its interior banger mechanism that provided a distinctive 'snap' sound. In later years the sweet was replaced within the cracker by paper hats, printed jokes and novelty trinkets; innovations introduced by Smith's son, Walter Smith. Today the tradition is still upheld, with crackers used as decorations both for Christmas trees and festive meals.

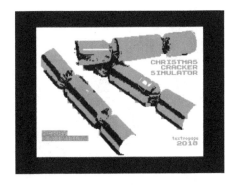

It may have seemed inevitable that such a long-standing yuletide tradition would eventually make the jump to the Spectrum, but in fact it took until 2018 before programmer Textvoyage (real name Neal Rycroft) decided to translate the after-dinner fun of the cracker into 48K of memory. Upon starting the game, the player is presented with a box of twelve virtual crackers. Upon snapping each of them, they are presented with a surprise item of questionable value (a plastic moustache, fortune-telling fish, etc.), a paper hat and a cheesy joke. Basically, that's it. The player can, however, run through the game again to see if the gifts and jokes are the same... and there is the major benefit of not having to clear up the detritus afterwards.

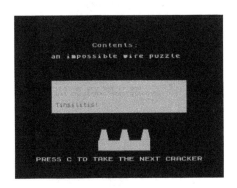

SCORE : 00000100

THE OFFICIAL FATHER CHRISTMAS GAME

Alternative Software (1989)

Here it is: truly the Rolls-Royce of Santa Claus games. While numerous other titles for the Spectrum purported to portray the Christmas Eve delivery efforts of everyone's favourite North Pole toymaker, only this game carried the official seal of approval from the man in the red suit himself. A budget title available for all three of the main 8-bit platforms, *The Official Father Christmas Game* also distinguished itself from other festive titles of the time in that its publishers donated a portion of the proceeds from the game's sales to Save the Children, the famous international charity which has been dedicated to supporting the lives of young people through improvements in health care, educational, economic opportunities and emergency aid since 1919. What was there not to like?

The game took place over three separate sections, with the player taking on the mantle of Father Christmas himself. In the first level, Santa must race through his North Pole HQ to collect all the parts of his sleigh and reassemble them in time for his Christmas Eve flight across the world. Unfortunately for Jolly Old Saint Nick, his elf workforce is in a playful mood and their japery has gone further than simply hiding all of the pieces of the sleigh; if Santa should collide with them, they will snatch back any components he has found and move them to another location. (The elves have a rather frustrating tendency to spawn from the edge of the screen at

the least helpful moments, usually right at the point where Santa is heading to the sleigh assembly point.) With only six screens making up the workshop, the action is never too taxing for very young players, but there is also a time limit to observe: if Santa can't get the sleigh reassembled before dawn, it'll be too late to get all of his other pre-delivery tasks sorted out ahead of the big day.

Get the rebuilt sleigh hitched up to the reindeer, and it's time for part two. In this section, the player compiles a list of gifts they would like to receive for Christmas (from a choice of fifteen goodies), and Santa then has to dash back and forth to collect the right selection of presents. The items drop vertically from the top of the screen, often at a fair rate of knots, so Father Christmas will find that his reflexes are given a bit of a workout. Thankfully the same items drop multiple times, so there are repeated opportunities to collect everything in good time.

Finally, part three sees Santa receiving a location to deliver the gifts he has just collected—there is a randomly-selected variety of four continents, each of them with slightly different architecture in evidence across the scrolling backdrop. With his sleigh flying high overhead, he must navigate each parcel through the air and into the highlighted chimney while trying to avoid them colliding with aircraft, birds and clouds. Thankfully there is a happy ending no matter how things play out: if Santa runs out of time, the elves prove that they aren't as bad as all that and will help out at the last minute to ensure that everyone gets the gift they wanted.

The Official Father Christmas Game was developed by Enigma Variations, a developer who produced numerous critically-successful original titles for the Spectrum such as puzzle game *Pipe Mania* (1990) and football simulator *Kick Off 2* (1990), but became similarly well-known for their tie-ins with kids' television shows which included *Postman Pat* (1988), *Sooty and Sweep* (1989) and *Count Duckula* (1989). Many of these games would also be published by Alternative Software, as *The Official Father Christmas Game* had been, and their extensive experience with family-friendly gaming fare certainly put them in good stead for this irrepressibly festive title. The icing on the cake was the game's large, appealing characters and detailed backgrounds created by legendary graphic designer Shaun G. McClure, who enjoyed a towering reputation in the software industry with a prolific career; dozens of games featured graphics and loading screens created by him over the years.

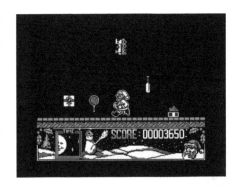

Alternative Software was one of the best-loved software labels of the 1980s, and—along with the company's main competitor, Mastertronic—it dominated the UK budget games market for many years. Established in the West Yorkshire town of Pontefract in 1985, Alternative rapidly built a large library of software between re-releases of previously full-price titles, many original games, and licensed adaptations of kids' TV properties which included several well-known franchises of the time. Although its gaming heyday came to an end in the mid-1990s, when users were gravitating away from 8-bit and 16-bit home computers in favour of desktop PCs, Alternative continued to diversify into applications and other types of software, meaning that the company continues to trade even today.

With its irresistible Christmas charm—from the jaunty rendition of 'Jingle Bells' which opens the game, through to the wintry refinement of its snowman-bedecked score counter at the base of the screen—it would be very difficult to say 'bah, humbug' in response to such a relentlessly cheery gaming experience. Yes, it is all a bit short, and admittedly some of the action is slightly baffling: doesn't six gifts per continent seem a bit stingy for the famously generous jolly old elf? But then you remember that the game was designed with young players in mind, and it becomes clearer why greater effort was expended on the yuletide ambience than perhaps was the case with cultivating addictive gameplay. It may not be a gaming masterpiece, but as a Santa simulator it ticks all of the necessary boxes.

WINTER SPORTS

Electric Dreams (1985)

The winter sporting compilation became something of a subgenre on the Spectrum in the eighties, and *Winter Sports* was one of the earliest examples—a multi-load anthology which encompassed eight different events which included downhill skiing, slalom, giant slalom, ice hockey, ski jumping, speed skating, bobsled and biathlon. Surely enough variety to have even the most seasoned enthusiast reaching for their snow-goggles!

Programmed for the Spectrum by game designers Software Images, who had also been responsible for the movie tie-in adaptation *Back to the Future* in the same year, *Winter Sports* was published by Electric Dreams—a software house with an excellent catalogue of titles which remains fondly remembered for its two wildly different takes on James Cameron's sci-fi horror film *Aliens* (1986) in both 1986 and 1987, top-down maze-based adventure *Dandy* (1986) and the immaculately-designed but frustratingly precise puzzle game *Spindizzy* (1986). *Winter Sports* was typical of the company's polished line of products, though it was to meet with a decidedly mixed response from reviewers.

The game's eight event line-up was ambitious, but the playability was to vary wildly between one stage and another. Where it arguably succeeds best is in its presentation of events such as ice hockey, which were less common fixtures in winter games compilations than other subjects such as skiing and skating. The player controls a six-person team which have four short, timed sessions to beat their opponents; the game moves smoothly with the player always taking control of the character closest to the puck, and an aerial layout at the top of the screen shows the placement of both teams on the rink. The inclusion of the event felt a bit like a breath of fresh air given general expectations of more established winter sporting activities, but it was not the only innovation that was on offer.

The ski jumping is presented well, with the player being given only a matter of seconds to gauge their character's approach to the slope, align their launch and then land safely. This fast pace nicely reflects the skill involved in the actual sport, and mastering the technique in the time allotted can be a challenge. Of the skiing events, the downhill skiing, slalom and giant slalom are all presented in a fairly similar way and involve the player navigating left and right as they chart their course and try to stay on track to gain the maximum number of points; the left-hand side of the screen shows a first-person perspective of the descent, while the right-hand side is given over to an overhead view. Speed can be varied in order to ensure that the player can angle themselves suitably to make their way along the course successfully by passing through each gate with precision.

A similar technique is used in the bobsled level, though the action is more frenetic and succeeds in presenting a more rewarding experience. More than ever, time is of the essence. Speed skating, by contrast, involves much joystick waggling as the player attempts to keep their velocity steady over a range of courses—each of different length. The joystick is also abused in the final event, the biathlon, where cross-country skiing takes the player across a frozen landscape as they make their way from one firing range to the next; targets must be shot with a rifle before tackling the next stage.

With speech synthesis in the menu screen, redefinable keys and a choice to play against the computer or a human opponent, *Winter Sports* presented plenty of class, though the variable quality of the subgames meant the critics sometimes opined that it was less than the sum of its parts. That said, for a sporting compilation there was still plenty of entertainment to be had.

CRIMBO: A GLOOP TROOPS TALE

Little Shop of Pixels (2010)

Santa is facing a nightmare worse than the time Mrs Claus accidentally sent his famous red suit to the dry cleaners on the 23rd of December. His mischievous elves have decided to go on strike, and have hidden Christmas presents all around Santa's North Pole residence. Now he has no choice but to track down every last one of them before he can deliver them to the children who are waiting expectantly around the globe for his arrival. (Thanks for nothing, elves—I wouldn't hold my breath for that pay rise.)

The Gloop Troops were colourful characters created by Little Shop of Pixels, appearing in a trilogy of platform-based action titles which began with the eponymous *Gloop Troops* (2010) and concluded with *Gloop Troops: The Lost Crown* (2011). *Crimbo: A Gloop Troops Tale* was the middle instalment, and the only one of the games to deal with a Christmas setting. Given that *Crimbo* features Santa as its playable character, it's actually hard to know exactly where the Gloop Troops are supposed to fit into the action as the only similarity is the fact that the games share largely a analogous style of gameplay. But it's Christmas, so let's just take it in our stride.

Crimbo's designers—Simon Franco, Andy Oakley and the enigmatically-monikered 'AJH'—do a great job of providing variety across the game's ten playable screens, with the action becoming progressively more difficult with each successive level. The characters are large and colourful, and suitably festive in nature—Santa must dodge hazards such as rogue Christmas trees and giant ice cubes if he is to collect all of the wrapped gifts safely. The game's collision detection can be a bit unforgiving at times, though thankfully our bobble hat-wearing hero is capable of jumping quite high and over fairly long distances, which gives him an edge when it comes to avoiding his opponents. The bad guys sometimes follow unexpected trajectories, especially in the later levels, so Santa needs to stay alert lest he find himself colliding with something nasty out of the blue.

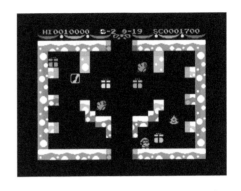

The 128K version of the game features some excellent music too, with an atmospherically festive ditty striking up on the title screen while the main action takes place alongside a jaunty rendering of 'The Sussex Carol' (sometimes better-known as 'On Christmas Night'), marking one of the very few occasions where the action of a Spectrum game is accompanied by the sound of a 17th century Christmas carol!

While the game's visual style is reflective of earlier platformer legends such as Ocean Software's *The New Zealand Story* (1989) and *Rainbow Islands* (1990), it very much has a style all of its own with the designers creating an entertaining, Christmassy environment which is brimming full of visual appeal. The action will involve a few very precisely-timed jumps and quite a bit of out-of-the-box thinking if Santa wants to make it to his sleigh intact, but with such an impeccably-judged difficulty curve the game never becomes a chore to play.

Nobody would say that the premise of *Crimbo* is bursting with originality, but Little Shop of Pixels take a well-known formula, dusts it down and gives it a fresh lick of paint for retro gamers to enjoy. The result is a game that would have surely become a festive favourite back in the eighties heyday of the Spectrum, but with its abundance of jovial charm it remains a highly engaging slice of item-collection action which retains the best of the format for the entertainment of modern audiences.

A SPELL OF CHRISTMAS ICE

Star Dreams (1984)

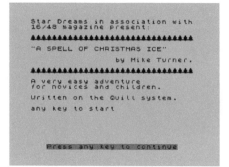

It's all kicking off at the North Pole—and just in time for Christmas! A malevolent ice witch has invaded Santa's workshop and cast a spell on the jolly old elf which has frozen him in a block of ice. The player has been transported to the top of the world in order to find a way to defeat the witch's magic, defrost poor old Father Christmas and get him back on track for his festive deliveries before time runs out. Failure will lead to millions of children across the globe being bitterly disappointed on Christmas morning... and presumably Santa being in dire need of a hot water bottle.

A Spell of Christmas Ice was written with Gilsoft's *The Quill* text adventure development system, and first appeared on Issue 12 of the *16/48 Tape Magazine*. The game was produced by Star Dreams Software and designed by Mike E. Turner, who was responsible for a number of interactive fiction titles on the Spectrum which included the innovative *Aural Quest* (1984), dreamlike mystery *The Sandman Cometh* (1984) and fantasy adventure *The Wizard of Tallyron* (1986). *A Spell of Christmas Ice* differed from his other games not just in its yuletide theme, but also in the fact that it was very much geared towards the younger adventurer. As such, the parser was considerably more streamlined than many other interactive fiction titles of the time; the game relies on a simple range of commands to engage with the action, which makes it particularly suitable for novice players.

The game itself is actually fairly short, and features a relatively modest map of locations within which the narrative plays out. There are many items that will be familiar to text adventure aficionados—a torch, a magic wand, a key that unlocks a trapdoor, and so forth—so certainly there are few surprises from a gameplay point of view. Where the game really succeeds, however, is in the frosty atmosphere that it evokes in its depiction of the North Pole. The player is called upon not just to find Santa's location but also to explore the wider area around his workshop... which includes some timeworn adventuring tropes such as a mysterious cave, a dark cellar, and of course the ice witch's blood-chilling lair. (Just be sure not to annoy her familiar, a black cat, or there will be unpleasant consequences to face.)

The strange stylistic choice of black text on a cyan background can prove a little headache-inducing after a while, and like many other interactive fiction titles of the same period there are no illustrations to accompany the prose. However, in this instance it works to the game's advantage as the text encourages the imagination of younger players to conceive of the kind of big-budget evocation of Santa's workshop that the Spectrum's graphical capabilities would have struggled to depict.

The action culminates in Santa's great hall, where the player must cast a counter-spell to thaw out not just Jolly Old Saint Nick himself but also his supporting band of toy-making gnomes (not elves, curiously—perhaps, given the grandeur of the North Pole setting, gnomes were all the software house could afford). Provided the player has collected (and is wearing) the required items they have uncovered in their travels, they may try their luck with dispersing the witch's malicious magic. But will the player succeed, or is Santa set to remain frozen until the end of the next ice age?

A Spell of Christmas Ice may not be the most challenging text adventure you will ever play, but it has plenty of good festive cheer and even—ironically enough, given the subject matter—no shortage of genuine warmth.

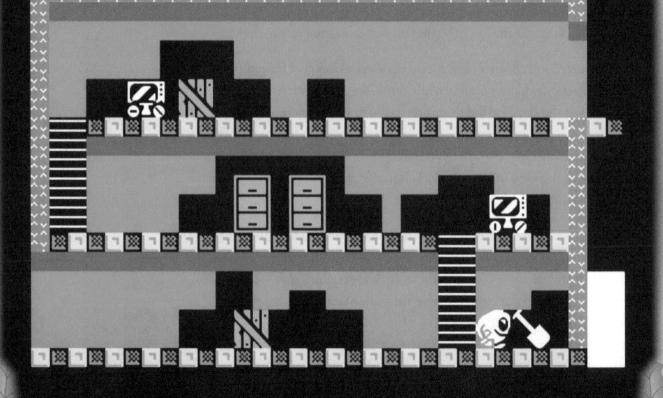

CHRISTMAS CRACKER

Eurogamer (2007)

There are few more time-honoured 8-bit traditions than the exclusive Christmas game, and it's heartwarming to know that the convention didn't end with the last of the Spectrum magazines disappearing from newsagents' shelves back in the early nineties, taking their cover-mounted treats with them. *Christmas Cracker* was produced by Spectrum gaming legend Jonathan Cauldwell exclusively for Eurogamer, the celebrated British videogame website which was formed in 1999, and is the closest thing you're likely to find to a cover-mount cassette in the digital age we live in.

Christmas Cracker featured (as the egg-cellent pun in the title might suggest to those in the know) the return of Egghead, the jovial ovoid character created by Cauldwell in 1989. Ever since his initial platform-based outing *Egghead*, which first appeared on the covertape of issue 73 of *Crash* magazine, the intrepid egg has made regular forays onto Spectrum screens over the years, with his hard-boiled adventures including *Egghead to the Rescue* (1990), *Egghead in Space* (2003), *Egghead Round the Med* (2007), and—most recently—*Egghead Goes to Town* (2017). Now something of an icon to Spectrum retro gamers, the character's success has been difficult to egg-nore, while his longevity has proven hard to beat. (It's okay; I'll stop with the egg puns now. And that's no yolk.)

The game's premise is pretty straightforward. Egghead must infiltrate the Eurogamer offices and rescue the website's team of journalists. This is achieved through a mix of exploration and jumping over any obstacles that might appear in his path to hinder his progress—including a sight familiar

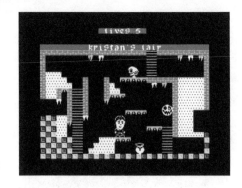

to anyone who went to school in the eighties; namely a TV that trundles along on wheels.

The game follows the fairly conventional rules of platform action titles (no real surprise, given that Cauldwell is the author of the acclaimed *Arcade Game Designer* and a true master of the genre), but includes a few innovations such as the ability to collect a shovel and dig through snowdrifts to reach new areas. Egghead will need to judge his descent carefully though, lest he end up accidentally stranding himself in an inaccessible position—an outcome that may require a restart. The Eurogamer staff members are represented by large, detailed caricatures, and Egghead can 'collect' them as he goes along. However, not all of the journalists are equally easy to access, and some are located in places which are likely to have players scratching their heads in puzzlement as they work out how to reach them.

With nine playable screens, the game is very much a mini-adventure by Egghead's usual standards, but *Christmas Cracker* is nonetheless an enjoyable slice of festive platform action that is very much in the vein of golden age fare such as *Moley Christmas* (q.v.), both in action and plot. While the game lacks music or a loading screen, it is nonetheless a fun flick-screen endeavour which captures plenty of yuletide frivolity.

Jonathan Cauldwell is a home computing polymath, responsible for dozens of titles over the decades ranging from simulations to strategy games. Though he has become especially well-known for his platform action games, not least those starring Egghead, in more recent times he has become just as widely recognised for encouraging new games development thanks to his programming tutorial *How to Write Spectrum Games* and the creator tool *Multi-Platform Arcade Game Designer*. With a huge back catalogue, he has become widely recognised as among the Spectrum's most prolific developers with well over fifty titles to his name. As if being the creator of Egghead wasn't a cracking achievement on its own!

FREEZ'BEES /
FROZEN PENGUIN

Silversoft (1984)

In an interesting curiosity, this game has two titles for the price of one. While its box-art and advertising went under the name of *Freez'bees*, its loading screen instead offers the alternative title *Frozen Penguin*. Both, however, offered the identical subtitle 'Doing the Sno' Shoe Shuffle', which perfectly sets up the game's commendable tendency not to take itself too seriously.

Freez'bees is heavily influenced by *Pengo*, Coreland's Antarctic-based arcade title released by Sega in 1982 and later widely adapted for home computer formats. In that earlier game, the heroic penguin Pengo must slide ice blocks around a maze to crush the hazardous Sno-Bees before they have the chance to sting him. This general format is recreated in *Freez'bees*, though with a few extra twists to keep things interesting.

Taking control of a penguin, the player can either burn through ice blocks to pass through the area they previously occupied or can instead push them into oncoming enemies (presumably the titular 'Freez'bees'). However, the penguin is also able to electrify the boundary fence which runs around the outer edge of the screen, which will temporarily stun any enemy that happens to come into contact with it, while they also have the ability to destroy bee eggs frozen within ice blocks before they can hatch.

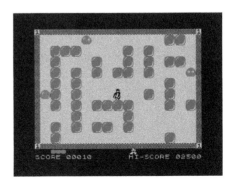

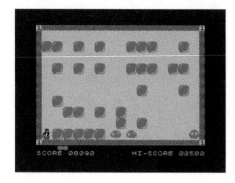

The game contains other elements of challenge—for instance, the random generation of the maze means that there is no way of forming any advance strategy from level to level, whilst the fact that the Freez'bees also have the capacity to burn through ice blocks adds an extra element of pressure on the player. The artificial intelligence of the opponents is very well pitched, and once a bee has latched onto the penguin's tail it usually takes some pretty fast action to shift it. The arcade-style spot effects are good, as are the suitably cartoony sprites, and the game also includes the neat ability to alter the speed of the gameplay. However, even on the slower settings the action still moves along smoothly, and there is plenty of replay value to be had.

Freez'bees was coded by David Leitch (who would later go on to high-profile arcade conversions for the Spectrum such as Melbourne House's *Double Dragon* and Virgin Games' *Shinobi* in 1989), and was published by Silversoft. This company produced games for the ZX81 as well as the Spectrum, and quickly established an eclectic and wide-ranging catalogue of titles which included platform game *Sam Spade* (1983), inventive ocean liner-based arcade adventure *Worse Things Happen at Sea* (1984), and Delta 4 Software's legendary J.R.R. Tolkien parody *Bored of the Rings* (1985). The company produced numerous other arcade conversions in its time, and *Freez'bees* was certainly among its most memorable.

At a £5.95 retail price, the game fell into something of a halfway house between a budget and premium title, but its appeal must have been obvious to the publishers as it was subsequently re-released several times throughout the decade by labels such as St Michael and the Prism Leisure Corporation as well as appearing on several compilation packs. While the bees may admittedly look more like amorphous blobs than hazardous insects, *Freez'bees* offers an enjoyable playing experience and certainly did an admirable job of translating frantic arcade fun onto the humble Speccy.

SANTA'S STRANGE DREAM

Textvoyage (2018)

Here comes Christmas Eve, and Santa Claus is clambering onto that famous sleigh again. Or is he? After a glass (or two) of pre-bedtime mulled wine, dear old Father Christmas has fallen into a slumber and is dreaming of his annual deliveries... except this time, there is a strange development. The dreamlike rendering of his sleigh-ride has been heavily influenced by the computer games of the early eighties, meaning that he is likely to encounter more than a glass of milk and some cookies on his journey.

Created by Textvoyage (a.k.a. Neil Rycroft), *Santa's Strange Dream* first appeared on *WOOT! Tape Magazine*'s second issue (the 'ZXmas' 2018 edition), and in many ways the game plays like a more refined version of his earlier title *Santa's Quick Drop* (2016). That Christmas Eve journey had been a much more conventional horizontally-scrolling evocation of Jolly Old Saint Nick's present delivery antics. However, with *Santa's Strange Dream* Textvoyage takes the concept into agreeably fresh territory—one which offers pixellated fun which takes the player right back to the earliest days of the Spectrum.

Over a series of levels, Santa flies across the screen on his way through a surreal landscape where Christmas trees can launch from the ground at a second's notice. Armed only with Rudoph's red nose laser (!) and the ability to throw parcels over the side of the sleigh at obstacles like festively-themed ballast, the hapless Santa must avoid increasingly surreal enemies such as flying Brussels Sprouts and soaring Christmas puddings as his night-time trek through the skies progresses.

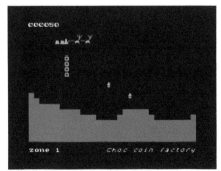

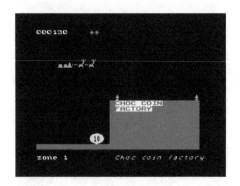

Written in Boriel ZX BASIC, the game certainly retains visual fidelity to the Christmas titles of decades past, and the action is pretty straightforward. Rudolph's nose-mounted laser can only shoot horizontally, whereas Santa's parcels drop vertically when thrown over the side of the sleigh (meaning that timing is crucial if they are to land on target). Bonus lives are awarded after certain levels are completed, which provides impetus to get to the end of every stage intact, and there is also the occasional extra item to collect here and there to increase the points total.

As might be expected given the game's deliberately retro experience, there is no musical accompaniment barring the odd bleep effect here and there, and the movement of Santa's sleigh and reindeer can be rather flickery as they scroll along. Similarly, the controls have a tendency to a be a trifle on the laggy side; as the game's instructions admit, the reindeer aren't the most aerodynamic animals on the planet, so they lack the ability to fly diagonally—thus leaving the player with only a rudimentary range of movement. However, rather than weaknesses in the game, these issues actually enhance the sense of faithfulness surrounding a playing experience which is supposed to feel a bit like a type-in program from an early eighties computer magazine.

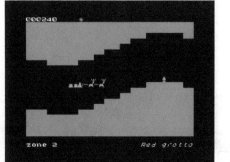

Textvoyage is something of a veteran of Christmas-themed gaming on the Spectrum, having coded numerous festive titles which include cracker-filling simulator *Cracfac* (2019)—which involves dropping novelty items from a production line into the interior of a Christmas cracker. His work is frequently tongue-in-cheek, but the wry sense of humour never obscures an obvious affection for the Spectrum's golden era and a determination to get the fine details just right to transport players back to the eighties and the formative years of home computing. *Santa's Strange Dream* may not be the most complex festive title ever to appear on the platform, but it exudes the kind of nostalgic appeal that will bring back happy memories of Christmas in the era of leg-warmers and Rubik's Cubes.

CRAPPY CRATES

The Death Squad (2016)

How would it be possible not to like a game called *Crappy Crates*? That title has a sort of in-your-face determination to be exactly what it says on the tin, and you have to admire it for its sheer audacity. (It's difficult not to think of Firebird Software's infamous 1985 compilation *Don't Buy This: Five of the Worst Games Ever*, for instance, which attempted similarly subversive marketing.) But fear not, for—in spite of its title suggesting that you lower your expectations a notch or two—*Crappy Crates* is actually rather good fun.

The action of *Crappy Crates* owes much to the Japanese NEC PC-8801 puzzle game *Sokoban* (1982), developed by Hiroyuki Imabayashi for Thinking Rabbit and later adapted for various 8-bit platforms such as the Commodore 64 and Apple II. In that seminal game, the player must push crates around a warehouse to ensure that they are covering particular marked positions on the ground: a task which may sound easy enough, but which rapidly becomes fiendishly difficult if they accidentally impede their own movement by shifting crates into places that block access to the right storage locations.

The Death Squad was to add their own spin on the *Sokoban* formula with *Crappy Crates*; this time around, a disembodied head must shove crates not by pushing against them, but rather by switching location as they come into contact with it—an innovation which sounds rather counter-intuitive, but one which becomes second nature soon enough. The player must keep their energy level topped up by collecting food items when they randomly

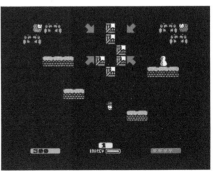

77

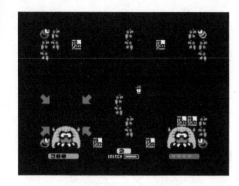

appear within the playing area—though they need to be quick as, in true *Pac-Man* style, the goodies will disappear within a set period of time. The crates themselves must be neatly stacked in an area indicated by a set of directional arrows before the stage is over. The player's progress is disrupted by the arrival of numerous enemies (from level three onwards) who are out to ensure that nothing runs nearly as smoothly as you might hope.

Each stage contains festively-decorated paraphernalia including sprigs of holly and snowy ledges, helping to enhance the yuletide ambiance. The sprites are generally large, brightly coloured and nicely detailed, lending the game considerable character and certainly helping to produce plenty of Christmas spirit into the bargain. Movement is smooth throughout, with the bare minimum of colour clash, and collision detection is admirably engineered.

The Death Squad was founded by the brilliantly-named Davey Sludge, and most of its titles have a distinctly scatological tone: consider, for instance, the less-than-subtly-named *Thunderturds* (2013), *Dung Darach* (2013), *Sewer Rage* (2016) and *Pooper Scooper* (2016). Thus *Crappy Crates* not only fitted neatly into the company's wider *oeuvre*, but also its general tendency towards puzzle-themed games. While it is currently the only Christmas game released by the developer, they were also responsible for the similarly-colourful Easter-esque *The Eggsterminator* (2018) and insect-oriented action game *Invasive Species* (2016). There is much to admire about the way that their highly professional approach to their craft is melded with a refusal to take themselves even remotely seriously.

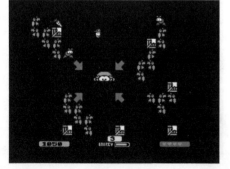

With level design that becomes progressively more challenging as the game continues, and a sagely-considered difficulty curve to guide you on the way, *Crappy Crates* is an entertaining playing experience which offers much to enjoy. It may not be the most conventional of Christmas games, but for a combination of action and head-scratching puzzles it shouldn't be missed.

THE MISER

River Software (1990)

It seems strange that, given how thoroughly embedded Charles Dickens' *A Christmas Carol* has become in popular culture, the ghostly festive tale has received relatively little exposure in terms of computer game adaptations. Since its publication by Chapman and Hall in 1843, the story of money-lender Ebenezer Scrooge's conversion from hard-hearted skinflint into a jovial and caring man full of warmth and humanity has been adapted countless times for radio, television and film, and yet the world of video-games has remained largely undisturbed by Dickens' yuletide literary titan. Perhaps the best-known version to date has been Disney's *A Christmas Carol* (2009) for the Nintendo DS, which won the Boysie Award for Best Movie Adaptation in 2009. But what is perhaps less widely acknowledged is that, many years beforehand, *A Christmas Carol* provided the backdrop for the action in *The Miser*: the Spectrum's very own take on the Dickensian tale, where River Software brought Scrooge and his acquaintances to life in the form of a detailed and frequently intriguing text adventure game.

River Software was founded by Jack A. Lockerby and produced interactive fiction titles between 1987 and 1995, including many innovative games which included *Lifeboat* (1987), *The Enchanted Cottage* (1988), *The Ellisnore Diamond* (1992), *The Dark Tower* (1992) and *The Civil Service* (1994). In the latter years of the company's life, Lockerby's text adventures were released through Zenobi Software. A prolific and skilled designer of interactive fiction, Lockerby produced some excellent titles during this period, and *The Miser* certainly ranks among his best.

One of the most interesting aspects of *The Miser* is that the game wisely assumes that the player will already be familiar with *A Christmas Carol* and its characters, and thus is able to commence the action *in media res*. Because we are all aware of Scrooge's misanthropic, tight-fisted character; that his hard-working but poor clerk Bob Cratchit is a warm-hearted family man; that Scrooge's nephew Fred despairs of his uncle's disdain for the festive season, and so forth, Lockerby wastes little time in setting the scene with incidents from the book. Instead, the game begins in Scrooge's bedchamber on Christmas Eve, where Jacob Marley's ghost has already warned his old colleague of the spiritual visitations to come and Scrooge knows that falling asleep will trigger a supernatural chain of events.

This is where the game diverges from Dickens' tale, as upon entering his slumber Scrooge is indeed visited by a Spirit of Christmas... but one who commands him to complete twelve good deeds in order to return to the human race. A fairly large hint soon presents itself in the form of a spectral visit to Bob Cratchit's home, where Scrooge's impoverished employee and his large family bemoan the fact that their economic situation leaves them unable to pursue their dreams of fulfilling various life goals. This is merely the start of Scrooge's task, however, as other opportunities await him around old London town to prove that he really is a reformed character who is ready to make a positive difference to the lives of other people.

Upon Scrooge's awakening on Christmas morning, the game opens up to encompass nineteenth century London—complete with some locations familiar from the Dickensian story, along with many which will be less obvious. Scrooge must identify every opportunity he can to perform a good deed wherever possible: something that is usually achieved by talking to non-player characters, deducing what difficulties they are experiencing, and then attempting to formulate a solution by collecting items from the surrounding locations and putting them into action to resolve the puzzle that has been posed. Only once Scrooge has successfully performed all twelve good deeds can he head for the home of his nephew Fred, resume his place amongst the living, and properly enjoy the Christmas celebrations for the first time in his life.

The Miser is packed full of Dickensian atmosphere, and while there are no images to illustrate the action, Lockerby uses every spare byte of the Spectrum's 48K to provide evocative text descriptions of the various locations and characters. The game was programmed by the use of Gilsoft International's *The Professional Adventure Writing System* (1987) and boasts a highly effective parser, though in truth it is rarely given a comprehensive workout as the puzzles are never excessively complex. Where the game excels, however, is in the way that it so successfully conjures up a wintry Christmas Day in Victorian London. This is not just a world of puritanical church services, starched collars and cosy Christmas dinners, but also of urchins working for scrap merchants, horse-drawn coal carts and characterful taverns. Lockerby does an excellent job of bringing this bygone world to life, filled with fascinating details in ways that enhance the extension to Dickens' story without ever competing with the original narrative.

The game pitches its difficulty level just right, as solving the game will require a reasonable amount of time and effort but none of the puzzles are overduly taxing. Most problems can be solved via common text commands such as 'examine', 'get', 'talk', 'say' and 'wait' (and, on one occasion, 'remember'), but there is enough variety from one conundrum to another that the player is unlikely to get bored helping Scrooge redeem his grasping ways by exploring his hitherto-unknown altruistic side.

Originally released at a budget price of £2.50 and re-released a number of times, *The Miser* provides excellent value for money and uses well-established text adventure conventions to produce a living, breathing world where Christmas is not just a celebration, but also a means of redemption.

SANTOS' CHRISTMAS ADVENTURE

Stonechat Productions (2017)

It isn't easy looking like somebody famous. Just ask Santos. He may have the white beard and the red suit, but he isn't feeling in the slightest bit jolly. Why? Because it's Christmas Eve, and he's been tasked with collecting all of the items for a perfect Christmas dinner, including the elusive golden bauble, or else his wife—the somewhat demanding Morag—won't even allow him back home. So Santos has little choice but to embark on this quest to gather every festive item needed for the big day... and not even an elf nor a reindeer around to help him.

Santos' Christmas Adventure is a platform action game in the grand tradition of titles such as Artic Software's *Big Ben Strikes Again* (1985) and Mirrorsoft's *Dynamite Dan* (1985). There are eight collectable items (ranging from a turkey to roast potatoes, dates and wine) spread across 21 separate screens—including, of course, the inevitable secret room. Like a cat, Santos has a total of nine lives to get him through the game, which is just as well as there are more than a few surprises awaiting him, such as obstacles that require a specific item to gain access to the area beyond.

As might be expected from designer Dave Hughes, the game is highly accomplished and contains many well-observed features; there are flying pigs in the air when Santos is exploring the clouds above his home, for instance, while there is a sardonic response for every item he collects (upon

82

grabbing the turkey, for instance, the player is met with congratulations on receiving a 'big, dry, tasteless hunk of protein'). *Santos' Christmas Adventure* was written with the *Arcade Game Designer*, and its cleverly-pitched difficulty level makes it accessible to just about everyone. The roaming enemies are well-realised, the main Santos sprite looks suitably fed up with his lot, and there is an admirable sense of general daftness surrounding proceedings which makes it well-suited for anyone looking for a bit of Christmas fun.

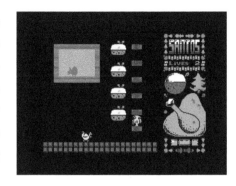

The 128K version of the game is accompanied by Matej Kovalcik's excellent rendition of Metallica's 1991 song 'Nothing Else Matters', which on the face of it may not seem like the most festive musical choice—but then, Santos himself isn't exactly brimming with yuletide *joie de vivre*, so in a way it's actually not as peculiar a musical selection as it might appear. The playing area is full of visual and environmental variety; no mean feat, given that the number of screens is reasonably limited. Santos can go soaring into the skies or explore subterranean tunnels, depending on the player's mood. Some jumps will require careful timing, of course, but it wouldn't be a Spectrum platform game without some pixel-perfect manoeuvres here and there—and with solid collision detection in place, it's a challenge that won't frustrate players for too long.

Such is the nature of life, Santos might just find that his Christmas doesn't quite go to plan even if he does manage to get all of the items together for dinner. Without spoiling the ending, the conclusion takes a pleasingly surreal turn for the metaphysical which proves curiously appropriate (if not necessarily all that agreeable) for the melancholic Santos.

With plenty of good humour, visual appeal and well-conceived game design, *Santos' Christmas Adventure* is worthy of anyone's time. For a quick blast of festive platform action, it certainly has what it takes to get the player into the Christmas mood (quite in spite of Santos' morose demeanour!).

CHRISTMAS PUDDINGS ATTACK

Textvoyage (2017)

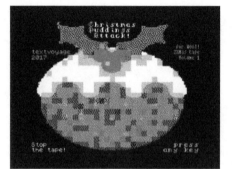

Christmas and shoot-'em-ups may not seem like natural companions, but Textvoyage sought to correct this misconception with *Christmas Puddings Attack*—a hybrid of festive jollity and wanton carnage that is perfect for anyone who likes a spot of holly and ivy with their *Space Invaders*.

The premise is that Earth is under alien attack.. at Christmas. Couldn't the extraterrestrials have chosen a more convenient date? Well no, as it happens, for a festive season incursion is all part of their dastardly plan. Having observed human traditions from afar, they decide to disguise their landing craft in the form of well-known Christmas items in the hope of blending in with their surroundings. Unfortunately for them, their sense of scale isn't quite what it might be, meaning that wave after wave of massively oversized yuletide paraphernalia attempting to land on the planet isn't all that difficult to spot.

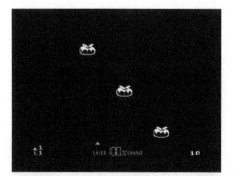

The player controls a laser gun which can slide from left to right across the screen. Once it is lined up against the invaders, it can be fired to repel the alien craft. However, accuracy is essential—only a direct hit to the centre of the invading ships will be sufficient to destroy them. The laser takes a few seconds to recharge, so timing is also a significant factor if all of the craft are to be wiped out. Should any of the aliens make contact with the Earth's surface, the player loses a life.

With each successive wave of ships, the invaders attempt a different form of camouflage: there are landing craft disguised as Christmas puddings, chocolate coins, roasted chestnuts and so forth. If the player should succeed in repelling a set number of craft, they will move onto the next level and receive a bonus life.

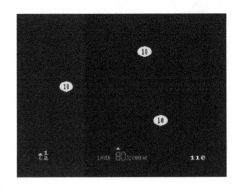

The descent of the various craft is perhaps not the smoothest scrolling you will ever see, but it is perfectly functional nonetheless. There is no background music—just a few bleepy effects here and there—but that seems entirely forgivable on account of the game's early eighties arcade feel.

Programmed by Neal Rycroft in Boriel ZX Basic, the game has a gleefully retro look, and the innovation of having to wait for the laser gun to recharge before its next shot introduces an additional aspect of time pressure which helps to make the experience at times feel a bit more like *Missile Command* than *Space Invaders*. With the seconds ticking down, there is an element of intricacy in lining up the laser to achieve a direct hit as there is rarely time for a second attempt. A glancing blow won't even leave a scratch on the landing craft, so a centrally-placed shot is crucial.

Whether the prospect of ever more outlandish Christmas goodies falling to Earth is quite enough to keep every player happy is of course a matter of personal taste; certainly there isn't a lot of variation in the gameplay as the player works their way through the levels, which may mean that this title isn't to everyone's liking. For an entertaining session of brain-in-neutral laser firing, however, the game certainly delivers (and then some).

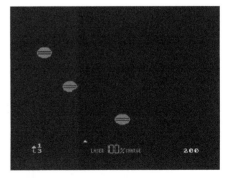

Nobody could reasonably claim that *Christmas Puddings Attack* was the most graphically sophisticated game ever to grace the Spectrum, but sometimes the simplest ideas are the most effective—and there is no taking away from the game its addictive appeal which resonates well with the recreated arcade origins of its action.

TIME	SPEED	RECORD
0:11.5		9:59.9

WINTER OLYMPIAD '88

Tynesoft (1988)

The 15th Olympic Winter Games, held in the Canadian city of Calgary in February 1988, was a landmark multi-sporting event which changed the world's public perception of winter sports. The first Winter Olympiad to be held over sixteen days, bringing the event into line with the Summer Games, Calgary set a new benchmark for winter sporting events—the games were widely televised, and with the host country sinking a record $829 million Canadian dollars into their organisation (more than any other Olympic Games at that point), expectation was high for the 46 events over ten separate disciplines which were held in the city that year.

Arriving just in time to capitalise on public interest in the Winter Olympics, Blaydon-based developer Tynesoft Computer Software's *Winter Olympiad '88* appeared on the market mere weeks prior to the Calgary Games commencing. The game was developed by Philip Scott and Derek Brewster, the latter being a well-known name on the Spectrum scene not just for games such as *Codename Mat* (1984) and *Kentilla* (1984), but also as a text adventure reviewer for *Crash* magazine.

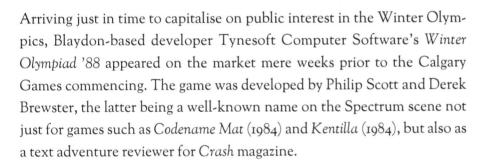

With various winter sports anthology titles already on the market, *Winter Olympiad '88* had its work cut out from the start when it came to establishing itself as one of the genre's big hitters. For one, it contained a relatively paltry five events in the form of downhill skiing, biathlon, bobsleigh, ski jump and slalom. Given the huge success of Epyx's *Winter Games* (q.v.) two years earlier, it was clear that the game would have to make an immediate impact if it hoped to distinguish itself among its competition.

After the player selects the nation they wish to compete for, there is a short opening ceremony and then it's straight into the action. The first event, downhill skiing, is arguably the most fast-paced section—the player can veer left and right as they descend a snow-covered slope, and must avoid trees while jumping over fallen logs which litter the course. Speed can be controlled, however, which can be helpful when negotiating sharp turns.

Next, the biathlon offers a combination of left-and-right joystick waggling to get the player through the skiing stages, interspersed by shooting a rifle at targets at various stages. Once this has been achieved, it's off to an ice track for the bobsleigh. The player will want to get a decent speed up as soon as they leave the starting point, as maintaining a fine balance of high velocity and good timing will be necessary to negotiate the various bends which are located throughout the track.

There is a change of tack with the ski jump, where style and technique take centre stage rather than speed. The player will need to pay just as much attention to their stance as to their safe descent from the slope if they are to impress the judges. Finally, the slalom involves descending a snowy incline on skis by weaving between strategically-placed poles on the way down; only a perfectly-calculated performance will win the day.

Winter Olympiad '88 sharply divided critical opinion in the trade press when it was released, with reviewers finding fault in the game's requirement to load every stage separately (*Winter Games* had loaded several events at a time), lack of variety when it came to music and sound effects, counterintuitive controls, and the occasional bug (which, as some reviewers commented, was suggestive of the game being rushed out to hit the market prior to the actual Winter Olympics taking place). But on the plus side, the game's graphics were widely praised, the presentation was generally recognised as being solid enough, and many approved of the sprite animation. It may have been a mixed bag, but the game still offers much to enjoy.

CRIME SANTA CLAUS

ETC Group (1996)

Poor old Santa Claus. It seems that Christmas Eve is never able to pass by without him suffering some mishap or other as he gets set for his big worldwide gift delivery. In *Crime Santa Claus*, it turns out that it's his magic staff that has gone missing—no, not the elves on his payroll that look after his North Pole workshop, but rather the enchanted cane he uses to allow him to magically enter people's homes to deliver their presents. Having no choice but to track down the errant item, will Santa be forced to rely on a bit of breaking and entering to achieve his goal (not recommended behaviour, even for someone who climbs down chimneys for a living)?

Taking place across 24 playable screens, *Crime Santa Claus* is an action adventure which was—visually and stylistically—very close in nature to the popular Codemasters games of the eighties such as the *Dizzy* and *Seymour* games. Santa must collect various objects from around the playing area which he can then use in conjunction with other items, or else give them to non-player characters in exchange for help (or a new object). Sometimes new areas will become accessible, so the player will need to stay vigilant. Similarly, their health level will decrease if they make a mistake in their actions, so it's safest to leave experimentation to a bare minimum.

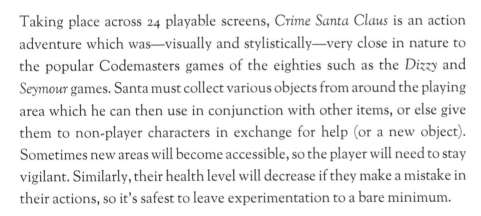

The game was the work of Ukrainian-based ETC Group, a collaborative effort involving the input of coders named Panda, Double Soft, Ticklish Jim and KT-Soft. Aside from the title, which is visible on the lower third of the screen next to the player's number of lives, the game's action takes place in Russian—a fact which has limited its accessibility in other markets,

and certainly makes things rather challenging to engage with if the player can't speak the language. Anyone overcoming that hurdle, however, will find a cleverly-designed and well-constructed game which certainly recreated some aspect of the charm of arcade adventures past.

The game's sprites are detailed and brimming with character, with the main Santa figure moving smoothly between screens, while the backgrounds present a good mixture of retro nostalgia and a willingness to push the Spectrum's hardware that little bit harder. The game's Eastern European influences crop up not only in the various characters' dialogue, but also in some of the distinctive locations that Santa encounters on his journey.

The action kicks off to the sound of a very respectable rendition of 'Jingle Bells' on the 48K version of the game, and a rather more complex original musical accompaniment on the 128K edition which contains plenty of festive jollity to get things started. (In both versions, the actual in-game playing experience is curiously silent.) However, perhaps the greatest attraction of the game is in its tongue-in-cheek moments—the shifty security agent lurking around outside the Kremlin, or the unconventional uses for the various items as Santa attempts to solve the puzzles facing him.

The adventure continued the following year in *Crime Santa Claus: Deja Vu* (1997), which was coded by BrokImSoft and Rush I.S.P.A.—groups which were both based in Ukraine. Developed in the Russian language, as the original had been, the sequel featured even more detailed graphics and continued the somewhat offbeat theme of Santa reluctantly flirting with criminality (as the title screen, featuring Father Christmas pinned down by a police S.W.A.T. team, gleefully demonstrates).

Crime Santa Claus may well be fated to be one of the Spectrum's more obscure Christmas outings, but for those willing to challenge the language barrier it proves to be a slickly-produced yuletide diversion.

SNOW JOKE

Delbert the Hamster Software (1991)

I'm sure it's happened to the best of us: you set off in your car on an ill-advised winter journey, only for the engine to stall at the worst possible point. Now you're trapped in a snowy countryside location, with no passing traffic and bad weather continuing to set in. All you can see from the windscreen is an endless rural vista of snow and ice. It's the early 1990s, so mobile phones are not yet the ubiquitous commodity they have become today... meaning that a quick call to a breakdown service for help is out of the question. With the car's doors frozen shut by the low temperatures and the engine steadfastly refusing to start again, what is your next move?

Snow Joke is a winter-themed exponent of one of the great genre novelties: the single-location text adventure game. In the grand tradition of inventive titles such as Zenobi Software's *Behind Closed Doors* (1988), all of the game's action plays out in one single place—and bereft of exploration, which is one of the most prominent aspects of interactive fiction, all of the emphasis is placed on problem solving. The result is a challenging and claustrophobic experience which contains plenty of good humour as the player seeks to escape the confines of their car... if only to emerge into the freezing cold elements which lie beyond it.

The game was designed by the enigmatically-named The Spud—the pseudonym of programmer Scott P. Denyer, who was a prolific author of text adventure games throughout the early nineties. Denyer produced interactive fiction titles including the *Arnold the Adventurer* trilogy (1990-92), *Star Flaws* (1991) and *Brian and the Dishonest Politician* (1992), with his games usually featuring quirky situations, inspired puzzles and a slightly offbeat premise. *Snow Joke* was no exception, as the game managed to pack a surprising amount of atmosphere into its one glacial but seemingly mundane location to produce the kind of playing experience that everyone could potentially relate to.

Designed with the *Professional Adventure Writer System*, the game encourages the player to thoroughly investigate the confines of their cramped environment in order to find any objects that may aid in their attempted exit from the car. Thus the various seats of the car, the steering wheel and glove compartment, the floor and so forth must all be examined in the hope that some useful objects may be discovered as a result. The car's boot is accessible via a panel behind the back seats, for instance, but the metal plate is securely screwed in place... so how can it be removed? And is there even anything useful to be found in the boot in any case?

Some of the items have functions which are self-explanatory: a heavy duffel coat on the passenger seat stops the protagonist from contracting pneumonia when worn, for instance. Others are slightly more obscure. At one point, ice must be melted in a container and the resulting water heated in order to defrost the car keys and allow them to be removed from the ignition, which in turn means that the keys can be used to unlock the glove compartment and liberate its contents. Sometimes commands must be slightly more precise than usual for a Spectrum text adventure: for instance, examining the passenger seat and examining *under* the passenger seat will yield different results.

Snow Joke contains few real narrative surprises, and anyone expecting a startling out-of-left-field twist at the conclusion will be disappointed. For a pleasant, puzzle-focused experience with a definite frosty ambience, however, the game is more than enjoyable enough to while away an hour or two.

COLIN'S CRIMBO CAPER

Stonechat Productions (2016)

When it comes to saving Christmas, when Santa Claus isn't available, Rudolph is recharging his nose and the elves are all busy with last-minute toy-building, there's really only one choice... and that's an amorphous blob named Colin. He may seem an unlikely kind of hero, but Colin is all that's standing in the way of all-out yuletide disaster. Over a variety of levels, he must collect all of the seasonal items needed for a perfect Christmas celebration such as wrapped presents, roast chestnuts and Christmas pudding, and then escape to the next stage before his time limit runs out.

Colin can move left and right as well as jump, but—making life slightly more difficult for him—he is unable to climb down ladders, meaning that timing is crucial if he is to get all the way around each stage to collect everything before the vital seconds tick down on his counter. On top of this, each level has enemies which move at a slightly different rate, which adds a further element of challenge as the placement of each fall and jump must be carefully considered if Colin is to avoid losing a life and going right back to the start of the current stage.

According to the game's loading screen, the action of *Colin's Crimbo Caper* is heavily inspired by Stephen Cargill's early platform title *Sir Lancelot*, released by Melbourne House in 1984. Certainly many of that earlier game's attributes survive the modification process—among them the moving stairways, slightly dodgy colour clash and merciless collision detection. Yet *Colin's Crimbo Caper*, created by Dave Hughes, manages to transcend its origins as a mod of a much earlier game: the level design is inspired, the

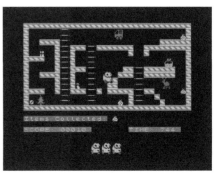

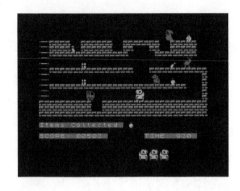

sprites are bold and detailed, and there is plenty of enjoyment to be had in beating the clock to escape each level in the nick of time. (Hint: discovering where the exit appears and planning your departure around its location is highly recommended if the player wants to make the most of every second.)

The action is slick, and certainly generates plenty of warm nostalgia for platform games of the past. There is no music to speak of—just a nondescript little ditty on the title screen—though there are occasional sound effects during the game. However, the game includes just enough inventiveness to set it apart from the dynamics of various other titles of the genre; the inability to climb down stairs, meaning that Colin must repeatedly find ways of dropping back to lower levels if he is to collect all of the errant Christmas items, can necessitate quite a bit of lateral thinking.

While the rampaging reindeer and menacing Christmas trees may seem like the villains of the tale, the real peril to overcome in *Colin's Crimbo Caper* is the time limit. Relentlessly ticking down as the player weighs up their path from one collectable item to another, the number of seconds spent waiting for enemies to shuffle around the screen to be evaded soon mounts up, meaning that Colin may find himself pipped to the post—falling short of reaching the exit by mere moments, and leading to him having to restart the level. Thus careful contemplation of each hostile non-player character's movements is important, as is giving Colin plenty of space to jump in order to evade oncoming enemies. A few attempts at each stage are therefore likely to be necessary... but as always, practice makes perfect.

Colin's Crimbo Caper first appeared on *WOOT! Tape Magazine*'s issue #0—the 'ZXmas' 2016 edition—and is a solid addition to Dave Hughes' expansive back catalogue of festively-themed games. With its appealing central character and plenty of Christmas cheerfulness, the game has no pretensions beyond presenting an enlivening runaround which will provide players with whimsicality and exasperation in equal measure.

CHRISTMAS GIFT HUNT

Stephen Nichol (2015)

It looks like even Santa's famous sleigh isn't immune to turbulence every now and again. There he was, off on his annual Christmas Eve journey around the homes of the world, and the next thing he knows the contents of his gift bag have been scattered to the four winds... or, more precisely, around the enigmatic Felliblanch Island. Now Santa has to explore the island to find all eighty of the presents that have fallen out of his sleigh—a task made considerably more difficult by the presence of hazards such as snowmen, toy soldiers and the malevolent Jack Frost, all of whom are determined to thwart his recovery efforts and keep the gifts for themselves.

Christmas Gift Hunt was created by Stephen Nicol with the use of the *Arcade Game Designer*, and was a maze-based action game based around item collection; with eighty separate gifts to track down, the player has their work cut out for them from the get-go. Felliblanch Island is an interestingly laid-out playing area, superficially rather visually samey (though the predominating Christmas colours of red and green are a nice touch) but actually concealing some very judicious layout design. For instance, patches of ice can only be crossed in one direction, and if Santa should need to reach the far side he has no choice but to find another way to access it.

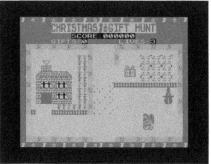

The game also makes good use of its antagonists; most will only walk back and forth in a set path, but Jack Frost is a rather more nefarious enemy and is capable of homing in on Santa's location which means that the player will need to choose their path carefully whenever they reach a screen where Jack appears. The game's setting is certainly capacious, with 54 separate

playable screens to explore. While the background graphics are basic, the sprites are large and exhibit plenty of festive appeal, while the playing experience calls to mind maze exploration games of the Spectrum's yesteryear such as Dollarsoft/Budgie Software's *Super Sam* (1985).

Nichol has produced numerous homebrew titles for the Spectrum over the years, among them text adventure *When Alex Didn't Do It* (2015), horizontal shoot-'em-up *Air Apparent* (2016) and platform game *Takeout Freakout* (2017), as well as the three-part *Cap'n Rescue* series (2014-16). *Christmas Gift Hunt* was an enjoyable addition to his catalogue of titles: while its design may seem minimal at first blush, the map is carefully constructed and the playing environment contains plenty of wintry charm—not least with the inclusion of its snowy range of buildings.

Nichol would return to the subject of Christmas the following year with *Christmas Magazine Hunt* (2016), a game which played almost identically to its predecessor. This time, in a nod to the fact that *Christmas Magazine Hunt* was written for inclusion in *WOOT! Tape Magazine*, the action takes a greater focus on printed matter: rather than searching for lost presents, Santa ends up losing eighty Spectrum magazines around Felliblanch Island while carrying out a delivery round to help a local newsagent. Now he must find every last copy and collect them so that they can make it to their intended destinations. Fortunately for Santa, the layout of the island remains the same—as does its line-up of opponents—meaning that he can focus his efforts on collecting errant issues of stalwart publications from yesteryear including *Your Sinclair*, *Crash* and *Sinclair User*.

Christmas Gift Hunt was by no means the most demanding Spectrum game, but it exhibits considerable festive joviality and serves up the player with plenty to explore and track down. Considering the amount of smoke coming from their chimneys, however, I don't think anyone could blame Santa if he gives the homes of Felliblanch Island a miss next Christmas Eve.

MERRY XMAS SANTA

Icon Software (1984)

It really must be a thankless task, being Santa Claus. Not only does he have to get around the whole planet in a single night, but even when he's making his deliveries there are umpteen hazards to contend with. Christmas Eve in 1984 is no different. Good old Father Christmas has to make his way across one slippery roof after another as he tries to distribute presents, all the while trying to avoid snowballs flying at him, falling icicles and belligerent snowmen. (Frankly it's a wonder the poor man doesn't jack it all in and tell everyone to order their gifts via home delivery instead.) Fortunately it's not all bad news, as there are culinary goodies to enjoy along the way such as Christmas cake and plum pudding—though Santa might just want to give the sherry a body-swerve if he wants to keep a clear head; the action on the rooftops is demanding enough without being tipsy into the bargain (and potentially hazardous to boot, given the co-ordination involved in getting down all those chimneys).

Merry Xmas Santa is a platform action game released by Gosforth's Icon Software, and its colourful graphics instantly invite comparison to greats of the genre such as Firebird Software's *Booty* (1984) and Parker Software's *Popeye* (1984). The game was released at a mid-range price point of £5.95 and was very much geared towards maximum accessibility in order to capitalise on the festive period of its release. Though largely ignored by the trade press reviewers of the time, the game was widely advertised and has a fair amount to recommend it; certainly the quality of its production immediately sets it apart from many other titles of the same period.

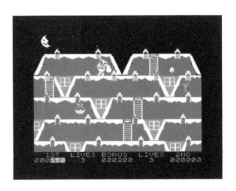

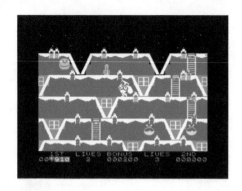

Control of the game is via joystick or the cursor keys, and players have the choice of playing alone or against another human opponent (taking turns rather than playing head to head). After a brief rendering of 'Jingle Bells', the action starts and Santa is deposited on a roof to start his deliveries. Once he has delivered presents to a home by passing its chimney, the chimney stack is highlighted in green; after he has successfully lit up every home on the screen, it's on to the next level.

Jumping gaps between roofs must be carefully judged, lest poor Santa takes a tumble and ends up in a painful heap. A far greater frustration, however, are flying snowballs which turn up out of nowhere; as they appear from the outside edge of the screen, it's impossible to avoid them if Santa happens to be standing close enough to the left or right of the playing area, as there is no time to even notice the snowballs' appearance—much less react to them.

The game doesn't contain all that much in the way of visual variety, though there are various pleasing touches such as Santa's personal observations which flash across the bottom of the screen, highlighted in purple. (He becomes quite excited if he comes across an Icon Software game amongst the presents being delivered to someone's house, for instance.) There are the usual bonus points to be had, of course, and collecting festive food where possible is always a good way of ratcheting up a high score.

Also active on the BBC Micro, Icon Software was one of the lesser-known developers of the Spectrum's early days, perhaps best-known for top-down maze game *Frankenstein 2000* (1985) and outer space-based platform title *Bug-Eyes* (1985). *Merry Xmas Santa* is one of their more widely recognised Spectrum titles, and certainly it holds its own within the well-populated field of platform/item collection games of the early eighties. While it may not offer the most varied gameplay by any means, there was always plenty of atmospheric Christmas fun on display.

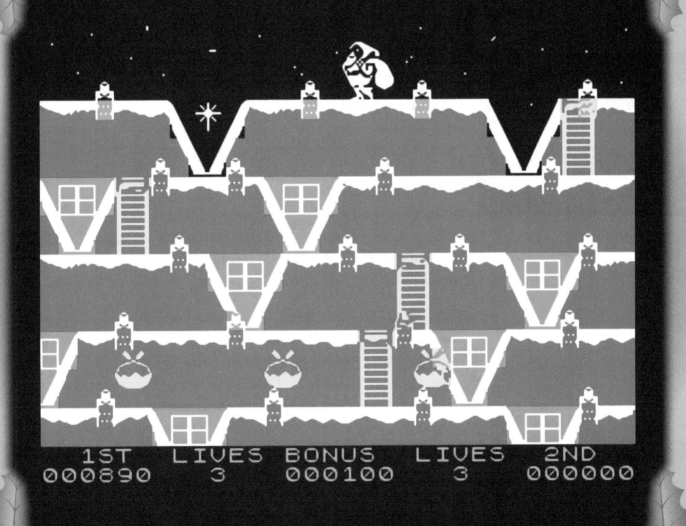

1ST LIVES BONUS LIVES 2ND
000890 3 000100 3 000000

THE SNOW QUEEN

St Bride's School/Mosaic Publishing (1985)

Based closely on the action of Hans Christian Andersen's 1844 fable of the same name, *The Snow Queen* is a text adventure game which follows the adventures of children Gerda and Kay as they overcome endless obstacles and adversity to thwart the machinations of the eponymous supernatural monarch. Told over seven chapters (a reproduction of the original tale is helpfully included by the publishers in the game's instructions), the story tells of Kay's abduction by the Snow Queen; perturbed by her friend's sudden departure and not even certain of his survival, Gerda must set out to locate him and safely return him to his home. Thus begins an undertaking that will eventually draw Gerda out of her familiar world and into a strange land of fantasy where anything can happen—and frequently does.

The Snow Queen was created by St Bride's School, one of the most consistently interesting interactive fiction developers of the 1980s. Better recognised for their anarchic text adventure games *The Secret of St Bride's* (1985), *Bugsy* (1986) and *The Very Big Cave Adventure* (1986), the County Donegal-based developers were celebrated by critics for their outlandish plots and absolute refusal to bow to convention. At face value, *The Snow Queen* appears to be a much more orthodox outing than their usual anarchic offerings... but, in true St Bride's style, there was plenty of innovation and unpredictable goings-on to be found along the way.

While some of the puzzles require close knowledge of the original material in order for the player to formulate a solution, other sequences have been crafted specifically for the game. Cleverly, the instructions explain that

Gerda encountered so many strange things on her travels, not all of them were chronicled at the time—and of course, if she should deviate from the intended events of the Andersen fairy tale then the whole course of the narrative might be altered as a result. Similarly, it is clarified that while Gerda is clever and resourceful, being a very young Danish girl she has some trouble with conversing in English (given that it is not her first language) and thus prefers to communicate in straightforward statements. To this end, the instructions list the game's possible commands (around forty or so in all) which not only gives an indication of the range of *The Snow Queen*'s parser but also inadvertently suggest a few clues as to how some of the puzzles might be tackled.

As St Bride's suggest, Gerda is very much her own person, and the strength of her personality is reflected in her resistance to some of the player's commands: if she feels that she is being asked to do something that is in conflict with her personal code of ethics, she will refuse. Similarly, she sometimes has to be persuaded that doing something is truly the right course of action before she will commit to it. While this might seem as though it might add a degree of inertia to proceedings, in actual fact it imbues the character with far greater personality and helps her to transcend the confines of Andersen's original characterisation.

Written with the aid of *The Quill*, *The Snow Queen* contains minimal graphical illustrations, though the background of the text will occasionally shift from cyan to magenta if emphasising a dramatic point. The game itself is split over two parts, with

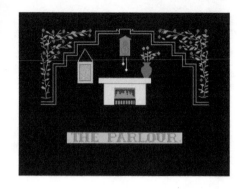

access to the second half of the game made possible by the use of a password which is whispered to the player at the conclusion of part one. While the puzzles seem geared primarily towards the younger player, some—such as escaping the magic garden in part one—are a little more taxing and will require some nonconformist thinking. While a lot of the solutions are suggested by the events of the Andersen tale, it always helps to remember the fantasy basis of the environment which opens up new possibilities that might not otherwise generally suggest themselves (talking to inanimate objects is sometimes required, for instance).

Reviewers in the trade press gave mixed appraisals of the game, being generally receptive to St Bride's presentation but often finding that the fairytale premise of the game was not to their taste. Some regarded the puzzles as being banal and unadventurous, while others took the exact opposite view and considered some of the solutions to be too obscure for younger players; the unexpected impact of the North Pole's magnetic field on compass directions, for instance, coming in for criticism. A number of commentators did point out that the icy setting of *The Snow Queen* would have made it the perfect game for Christmas, however, which made its decidedly un-seasonal midsummer release date somewhat baffling.

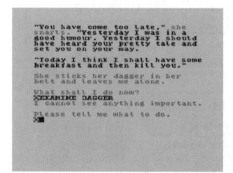

The Snow Queen is certainly a must-have for St Bride's completists, and anyone who enjoys a bit of out-of-the-box thinking will undoubtedly find a fair bit to entertain. It may lack the overt zaniness of the developer's more popular titles, but the game is an appealing curiosity not just for fans of literary adaptations but also as an early example of a strong female protagonist in interactive fiction. In the hands of St Bride's School, we are left in no doubt of Gerda's likeability and appeal, while her polite forthrightness and avowed independence of thought feel like a breath of fresh air. *The Snow Queen* may well be the most eccentric of fairytales, but the game is most assuredly none the worse for it.

SMILER'S CHRISTMAS SACK

Digital Prawn (2010)

Christmas celebrations are for everyone... even grinning disembodied heads. This is good news for Smiler, a moveable character who looks for all the world like one of those 1960s-era smiley face badges designed by Harvey Ball. Smiler must travel around a series of mazes (eight in all) collecting Christmas gifts, each of which is marked by a letter of the alphabet, then return to the home point on each screen. On the positive side of things, he is accompanied by his cousin Casper (who looks identical, but for the fact that he is red rather than yellow). But rather less convenient is that the maze is filled with arrows, and Smiler and Casper are only able to move in the directions they indicate—with no exceptions.

When one of the characters moves onto an arrow, it has an effect on the other arrows on the screen: magenta arrows will move other arrows ninety degrees clockwise, for instance, while red arrows will rotate all arrows anti-clockwise by ninety degrees. Thus it will take a fair bit of trial and error to not only collect the festive presents, but also to get both characters back to the home point (a condition for completing the level). However, the player can switch between Smiler and Casper at any time—usually in the hope that one character can save the other from being trapped by the directional arrows—and the level can be restarted as often as necessary. A sanity-saving access code is provided at the end of every level so that the player can start on the last stage they tackled rather than having to battle through from the beginning every time they play. Also, they must take careful note of the letters which denote each parcel, as they will need all of them to take a crack at the eight-letter anagram at the end of the game.

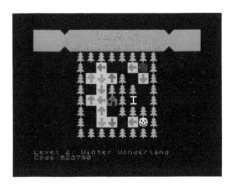

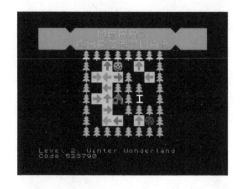

Digital Prawn has proven to be a prolific developer of indie games, being especially well-known for their 'one line' series—where playable games of many different genres (including maze exploration, arcade action, text adventures, puzzles and board games) have been created in a single line of code. However, they have also become synonymous with the *Smiler* series of games, beginning with *Smiler in Arrowe Land* [sic] in 2010, and continuing with *Smiler in the City* (2010), *Smiler Travels Around Blighty* (2010), *Smiler: Grinner on Tour* (2010) and *Smiler: The Scattered Ruins* (2010). All of the entries in the series employed similar (indeed, near-identical) graphics and game mechanics, and *Smiler's Christmas Sack*—the sixth and, to date, final title in the cycle—was no exception to the rule. Yes, there are Christmas trees, and the falling snow is a nice touch, but the game is very much in keeping with its predecessors... and none the worse for it, working on the old principle of 'if it ain't broke, don't fix it'.

The *Smiler* games were all programmed in the Z88DK Small-C development environment, and are very efficiently coded—though not without the occasional foible (as the creator notes in the game's instructions, the falling snow is interrupt-driven so it momentarily pauses whenever a sound effect plays!). There is little in the way of presentational trimmings, such as music or a loading screen, with the game simply launching straight into the action after the player has been presented with an on-screen list of keyboard controls.

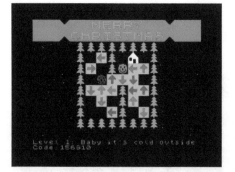

Whether players find *Smiler's Christmas Sack* a challenging or frustrating experience will depend entirely on personal taste. Certainly it seems inevitable that much use will be made of the restart command, as one single false move is all that it takes to accidentally trap both characters in unwinnable positions. If you're able to overcome the game's highly unforgiving level of difficulty, however, the puzzles come thick and fast. For a yuletide brainteaser, there is plenty of amusement to be had.

RALLY XMAS

Stonechat Productions (2016)

Have you ever wanted to play a game like *River Raid*, only taking control of a giant roast turkey rather than a jet fighter? (Now there's a sentence I never thought I'd write.) Well, if the answer to this rather out-of-left-field question happens to be yes, I have excellent news: *Rally Xmas* is almost certainly the game you've been waiting for all this time.

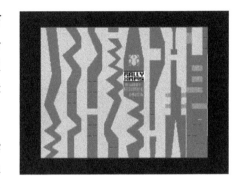

Programmed by Dave Hughes and first appearing on *WOOT! Tape Magazine*'s 'ZXmas' 2016 edition, *Rally Xmas* presents the player with a simple but fun experience: they must steer (!) their roast turkey along a winding stretch of road, which becomes progressively more twisty as their journey continues. As well as the odd narrow length of track, the turkey must jump to avoid obstacles: a short hop to negotiate low hazards, and a longer leap if they want to overcome larger dangers.

Hughes has planned the track to perfection, and players will need to stay on their toes if they expect to anticipate all of the hazards along the way. There is a definite 'one more go' quality to proceedings, as most will want to continue hammering away at their keyboard until they see the game through to its conclusion.

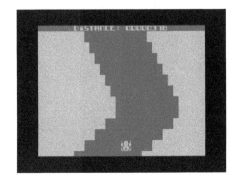

While it's true that the game's concession to the festive season lies entirely in its choice of a roast turkey as its choice of controllable vehicle, anyone who ever wanted a Scalextric set under their Christmas tree as a kid will no doubt feel right at home. Though by that same token, I can't imagine too many will be queuing up to cook a turkey that's just negotiated more hard turns than a rally car at Brand's Hatch.

THE GAMES: WINTER EDITION

Epyx/US Gold (1988)

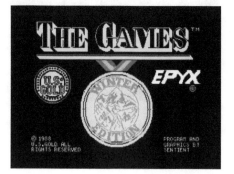

By the late 1980s, the field of Winter Olympics simulators had started to become rather well-populated on the Spectrum. However, in the eyes of many reviewers it seemed as though the best had been saved for last, as Epyx—who had been responsible for the well-received *Winter Games* (q.v.) some years beforehand—was to burst back onto the scene with this late-in-the-day anthology of snowy sporting events.

Converted to the Spectrum by Sentient Software (who would also be responsible for developing *The Games: Summer Edition* for the platform the following year) for Epyx, and released by US Gold, *The Games: Winter Edition* wisely combines everything that had worked previously with *Winter Games* along with many new events. This ensured not only that gameplay was immediately familiar and easy to pick up, but also that there was plenty of variety on offer—the collection comprised some entirely new sports along with others which were making a reappearance from the previous anthology, but presented in an entirely new way.

With up to eight different competitors able to take turns, and choosing a number of nations they can represent, the game allows players to compete in all seven on the events, to choose a selection of them, or just to practice a single one. It then wastes little time in catapulting the armchair sports fan straight into the first event: the luge. Perhaps the most infamous of winter sports—it essentially involves bodily careening along an icy track on little more than a metal tray—the game achieves an impressive sense of speed by repeatedly flicking from screen to screen as the player's character races down the route. The figure's position must be carefully coordinated on the track by making small but prudent moves, judging the drift rate as the player attempts to steer the character successfully. There are four different tracks to try out, each with their own challenges to overcome.

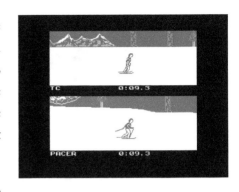

Cross-country skiing is the next event, and the player is offered three different tracks to choose from—each gradually increasing in length. It's then time to try their luck with that most time-honoured of sporting game skills: joystick-waggling. The character is controlled by a rapid left-and-right movement, and must negotiate various inclines if they are to beat the pacer (shown on the bottom half of the screen).

Next up is figure skating. This event plays quite differently in comparison to its earlier outing in *Winter Games*; the player is given a choice of music to accompany their routine as well as an opportunity to rehearse the various movements that appear in it, before taking to the ice rink in the hope of suitably impressing the judging panel. An on-screen indicator helpfully shows which jumps, spins and pirouettes are required to be performed at any given point, but success will depend on remembering how to break into the necessary movements at the right time.

Following this is the ski jump, where a good score will hinge on timing as well as position. The player sets off from the top of a high slope, then must carefully line up their skis as they progress downwards; hitting the fire button just as they reach the end of the track will make the difference between launching into the air and manoeuvring safely to the ground, or the player character simply falling flat on their face. There is, at least, a good sense of momentum to accompany proceedings; the various stages of the event speed by from different perspectives, which certainly adds a bit of

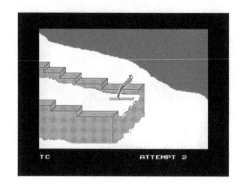

additional edge to the time pressure. It also manages to put a fair bit of clear blue water between this approach and the tack used in *Winter Games*.

The slalom takes an isometric, side-on view, where the player must race from right to left as they negotiate their way around a series of flags while trying to outrun the non-player pacer. Rapid responses will be necessary if the track is to be cleared proficiently without any collisions; hit a flag or stray too close to the edge of the playing area and the player character will find themselves heading for a tumble.

The speed skating event is, again, quite different from that which had been portrayed in *Winter Games*. Using an aerial view rather than the sideways depiction of its predecessor, progress depends on hitting the right rhythm of motion and avoiding the despondency of landing painfully on the ice. Waggling the joystick is once more the order of the day, but there is a welcome sense of complexity in not just upping the velocity but also ensuring the correct alternation of movements.

The last of the events—downhill skiing—takes a first-person perspective to depict its action, where the player must skilfully manoeuvre left and right to make their way between gates. While the unsophisticated blockiness of the graphics make this section seem slightly rudimentary in comparison to the other stages, the trade-off is that the level does at least move along rapidly, with the player having to anticipate not just the gates they are passing through but also the ones which are approaching from just beyond.

With opening and closing ceremonies, podium presentations for medals after every stage and some great music on the 128K version, *The Games: Winter Edition* is a polished package. Though its graphics are variable from one event to another, it never retreads too much familiar ground from its illustrious predecessor, and contains much in the way of frosty atmosphere.

WINTER WONDERLAND

Incentive Software (1986)

For those of us who are dreaming of a white Christmas, this one is most definitely a bit out of the ordinary. The protagonist of this text adventure tale is an anthropologist who, after ten years of research, is still waiting for their big breakthrough. However, when they receive a mysterious message from a colleague—a Russian archaeologist who is currently working in Tibet—everything looks set to change. Following up some curious reports of a lost civilisation based in the Himalayas which has developed at the same rate as modern society, though completely isolated from it, the anthropologist hires a Cessna light aircraft and heads off to their colleague's last known location. Alas, a snowstorm sets in just as the player's character is heading for the dig site, and they soon wind up crashing into the ice below. Now stranded in a snowy wilderness with no indication of their whereabouts, the hapless researcher has no choice but to explore the area and try to survive: their continued existence may well depend on being able to track down the lost civilisation before the elements take their toll. Finding safety, however, will largely depend on just how friendly the citizens of this isolated society turn out to be once they are encountered...

Part of Incentive Software's Gold Medallion range of interactive fiction titles—which also included games such as *The Legend of Apache Gold* (1986) and *Karyssia: Queen of Diamonds* (1987)—*Winter Wonderland* sold for the mid-range price of £7.95. The Gold Medallion titles were text adventure games that had been developed using Incentive's own *Graphic Adventure Creator*, and which were thought to demonstrate the best of the system's capabilities. Created by Simon Lipscomb and Tim Walsha, many of the locations are illustrated and successfully reflect the game's icy atmosphere.

The puzzles of *Winter Wonderland* are somewhat simpler than its complex scenario might otherwise suggest, though this has the advantage of making the experience accessible to novice players as much as the experienced adventure fan. An early encounter with a polar bear blocking the player's way, for instance, is easily resolved by firing a flare gun to scare it away— which, as luck would have it, is just about the only item to be found in the frozen wastes. Thankfully the build-up to finding the hidden civilisation of Shangri-La is mercifully brief, and subverts expectation by cutting through a lot of stereotypical wilderness survival tropes and getting the player right into the heart of this secluded culture. This is where the action gets more complex, for if the player was expecting a primitive society they will be amazed when they discover modern hotels, an upmarket shopping area and even a monorail system! Thus there is a fair bit of exploring to do before the player can attempt to escape back to modern life—along with the story of a lifetime (and all the material he needs for an academic paper).

Though the game had a reasonably large number of locations, reviewers lamented its sudden death scenarios and some frustrating lapses in the parser. For instance, 'wear' isn't recognised as a command, meaning that the protagonist automatically puts on a heavy fur coat when it is picked up but seems content to simply carry snow-shoes rather than put them on. Similarly, a rope can be climbed before it is even secured because 'throw rope' isn't considered a workable direction for the character to follow. Overcome these odd lapses, however, and there is a fair bit of enjoyment on hand. *Winter Wonderland* was not the most complex text adventure to be released by Incentive, but it has a genuinely interesting premise along with a disarming level of difficulty which will encourage players to delve into its mysteries until the point that they have reached its conclusion.

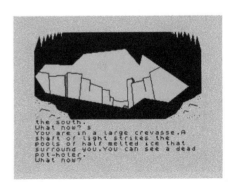

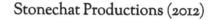

BAUBLE BLAST

Stonechat Productions (2012)

The premise of *Bauble Blast* is a simple one. Santa must take to a toboggan in order to scour the forests of the North Pole. Winding in and out between the fir trees are a plethora of mutated Christmas baubles, cruising along at speed. Santa must track down each one and shoot it into little pieces... but of course, it takes only one unfortunate twist of fate for the hunter to become the hunted, as a collision with any of the baubles will lose a life.

Bauble Blast is a maze game that, in its visual style, bears less resemblance to a *Pac-Man* clone than it does to titles such as Gem Software's *Oh Mummy* (1984). Designer Dave Hughes provides the gameplay with an estimable sense of speed; Santa will have to be agile with his toboggan if he's to shoot down all of the baubles without being caught by any of them himself. To this end, the game's artificial intelligence is pretty slick—not only do the baubles take sharp turns and evade fire, but they can quickly turn back on their present trajectory leaving Santa to make sudden evasive manoeuvres.

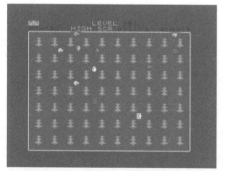

Bauble Blast was far from the most intricate game ever to be developed by Hughes: the sound is very basic (just a handful of spot effects here and there), and there is next to no variation in gameplay between levels which means that the player's motivation tends to be centred more around beating their own high score than it is with progressing through the game. There is an option to redefine the keyboard controls, however. All in all, the game is at its best when recreating some of the Speccy arcade-style classics of the eighties; it certainly does a great job of evoking the atmosphere of the addictive maze games of yesteryear.

SPECIAL DELIVERY

Creative Sparks (1984)

Do you remember those innocent days when Santa Claus' Christmas Eve deliveries seemed like a pretty straightforward plan? Father Christmas would jump into his sleigh at the North Pole, his bag bursting with gifts for the well-behaved children of the world, and thanks to the magic of the festive season he would make it all around the planet and back to his toyshop before the break of dawn. Well, as *Special Delivery* explains, this time Santa's plans have become a great deal more complicated!

Due to a faulty alarm clock, Santa finds himself in a right old pickle. Not only does he have just five hours to complete all of his deliveries, but the elves don't even have time to load up his sleigh with enough presents to give out to all the good kids around the planet. Thankfully some quick thinking from Jolly Old Saint Nick might just save the day: he contacts some angelic helpers who will collect wrapped gifts and distribute them directly to Santa's sleigh as he flies past. Sadly even that plan becomes convoluted, however, as if he collides with obstacles such as mountains or clouds then he will lose a gift from his sleigh. Similarly, touching a lightning bolt will cause him to lose an hour from his already restricted time limit. The demonic 'red devil' also gets in on the act, and soon starts dropping sabotaged packages of his own—if Santa accidentally collects one, it will cause him to lose one of the genuine presents.

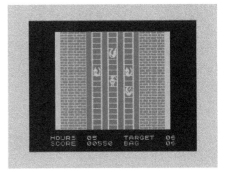

If Santa perseveres long enough, he will be able to deliver gifts to smaller houses by dropping them down the chimney when passing by. For larger properties, assuming that he has more gifts in his sleigh than the stated

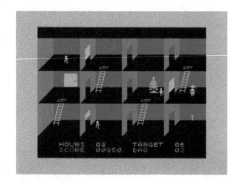

target, he must land on the roof, scramble down the chimney (avoiding an unfortunate combination of fireballs and snowballs) and place the gifts under the family's Christmas tree. In the process, he will need to avoid any sleepwalking children he encounters—more precious time will be lost if they should wake up—and then exit via the back door so that he can get back to his sleigh and continue his deliveries.

Special Delivery was published by Creative Sparks and programmed by Dalali Software—a developer who would achieve considerable success on the Spectrum with titles such as First Star's *Boulder Dash* (1984), Mirrorsoft's *Biggles* (1986), LucasFilm Games/Activision's *Rescue on Fractalus* (1986) and Piranha's *Yogi Bear* (1987). Initially a mid-range title retailing at £6.95 before being re-released at a budget price of £1.99 as part of the publisher's 'Sparklers' range, the game's Christmas theme—which at this early stage in the Spectrum's life was still something of a novelty—caught the imagination of several trade press reviewers of the time. With its suitably festive (if admittedly somewhat basic) graphics and a rendering of 'Jingle Bells' that will raise a smile for all but the most Grinch-like player, there was no doubting that the game was certainly crammed with yuletide charm.

Particularly at its budget price point, *Special Delivery* provided good value for money in that the game's different stages—both in the air and on the ground—complemented each other well. The action gradually becomes more difficult as Christmas Eve progresses, and younger players in particular will find the game to be a decent challenge rather than an uphill struggle. The game supported five different forms of joystick as well as keyboard controls, so there was no excuse for not diving straight in to give poor old Santa a helping hand. *Special Delivery* may not necessarily be to every taste, but—like all the best things at Christmas—taken in moderation there is a lot to enjoy here. For a slice of atmospheric Noël whimsy from the Spectrum's formative years, it comes highly recommended.

ELVIN THE ELF

ZXF (2006)

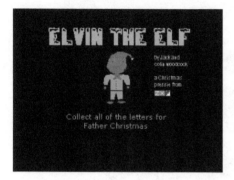

It's all work and no play for an elf. That's certainly the case for Elvin, one of Santa's dedicated North Pole workforce, who has been tasked with hunting down several letters to Father Christmas that have accidentally gone astray. He must make his way around Santa's toyshop collecting each piece of correspondence, then make sure that they are all delivered to that famous sleigh before time runs out. After all, nobody wants to see someone on the nice list having to go without a present at Christmas, do they?

In true *Manic Miner* style, *Elvin the Elf* follows a time-honoured format of progressing screen by screen with the only objective being the need to collect all of the necessary items before the exit appears... and then promptly departing for the next stage. There is a time limit, of course, which ticks down the seconds on each level (after all, the letters all have to reach Santa before he departs for his deliveries). Thankfully Elvin has a plentiful seven lives to see him through his exploits.

Elvin the Elf was developed by Colin Woodcock and Jack Woodcock, and was created using Jonathan Cauldwell's *Platform Game Designer* which was released by Cronosoft in 2005. The central sprite moves smoothly, and the letters are all placed in reasonably accessible places which means that there is a minimum of frustration involved in collecting them. With a total of only seven playable screens, it won't take too long for Elvin to make his way around the North Pole, though there are admittedly a few occasions where a misstep is enough to get him trapped (meaning that it is necessary to repeat the level to get him out of his predicament).

The Christmas iconography is bold and colourful, and certainly gets the most out of the Spectrum's palette. Music comes in the form of a looped rendition of 'Jingle Bells' which sets the scene nicely, though players may find themselves muting it after the umpteenth replay. The interface is very much in the spirit of platform games from the Spectrum's glory years, the only quibble being that the initial instruction of 'press any key to start the game' remains onscreen throughout the action and is partially obliterated by Elvin's lives meter.

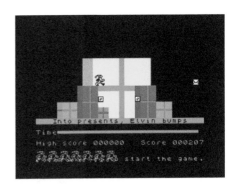

With its limited number of stages, *Elvin the Elf* is more a bit of festive fun than a gameplay marathon, and most players will make their way through it in fairly short order. It is, however, especially entertaining for younger users who will no doubt enjoy the welcoming recreation of Santa's workshop with all of its charm and idiosyncrasies. The time limit set for each level is more than humane, and with so many lives at Elvin's disposal there is plenty of potential for an enjoyable meander around the magical Christmas land that the game conjures up.

When it comes to yuletide platformers, *Elvin the Elf* certainly ticks all of the boxes in terms of festive imagery: it's all up there on the screen, from crackling fireplaces and piles of presents through to snowmen, angelic Christmas tree toppers and even a giant cracker. Adding to the general sense of amiability, every level is designated by a descriptive line which forms one half of a rhyming couplet; you'll need to get through the whole game to read the poem in its entirety.

Making your way around the various stages of the game may contain little in the way of genuine surprises—there are few occasions where pixel-perfect jumps are required, for instance—but *Elvin the Elf* is full of pleasant little details which can't fail to raise a smile. Let's just hope that Santa remembered to give his faithful assistant a pat on the back for his hard work; after all, it's important to consider the elf-esteem of your employees.

GRUMPY SANTA

Paul Jenkinson (2017)

Santa Claus may otherwise be known as the Jolly Old Elf, but with the pressure of expectation on his shoulders you could certainly forgive him the odd lapse in his sanguine nature every now and again. That was certainly the case in 2017, when all he wanted was to get the world's presents delivered and then head home to relax with a glass of sherry... only to discover that a malevolent bunch of snowmen and their henchmen—some belligerent elves—had stolen the gifts and hidden them across a wintry landscape in a bid to ruin Christmas. No wonder Santa gets fed up with this kind of thing.

His patience sorely tested, Santa must set out across the frozen wastes in a bid to get all of the presents back. Only once he has collected every last missing gift will Mrs Claus let him into the workshop so that he can unwind with a drink in front of a warm fire. Every level is contained to a single screen, and each present appears in four separate quarters—only by assembling the complete gift (which appears at the bottom of the screen) will the exit from the current stage materialise and let him progress further into the game.

The presents pile up at the bottom of the screen, indicating how far Santa has reached in his quest. Some judicious jumping from platform to platform will be required to evade his marauding opponents, and with only three lives available he'll need to be careful as there are a total of 22 screens to get through. The environment gradually changes from frozen caverns and a snowy forest to the the chilly lair of the snowmen themselves, meaning that the game certainly demonstrates a reasonable amount of visual variety along the way. After the first eleven presents are collected, Santa is sent on to pick up another batch in the slightly more challenging second half of the game, so there's no rest for the wicked... or even the jolly.

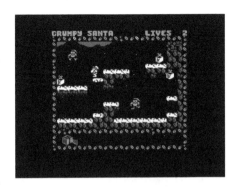

Created by Paul Jenkinson in the *Arcade Game Designer*, *Grumpy Santa* bears plenty of similarity to his *Toofy* range of games—and is none the worse for it, as the sprites are detailed and full of character, while the difficulty level is fairly benignly pitched throughout. The game is strangely devoid of music, which seems like a bit of a wasted opportunity (especially on 128K versions of the Spectrum), but there are simple effects to accompany various actions. On the plus side, the game's controls are very simple—just left, right and jump—with no fussy convolutions, so players know they are being served up with a slice of platform action that hits the ground running and just keeps on going.

While the platform-based collect-'em-up wasn't exactly an original concept for a Christmas game, Jenkinson brings enough seasonal allure to *Grumpy Santa* to keep most players interested. There is undoubtedly a sense of curiosity at slowly delving into the realm of the snowmen and seeing what he has devised by way of inventive backgrounds (complete with Christmas trees and so forth) before the game reaches its climax.

Although Jenkinson has been a prolific developer for the Spectrum, with his well-regarded output spanning many genres including text adventures and arcade action titles, he has become especially widely known for his platform games such as *Antiquity Jones* (2012), *B-Squared* (2017), *Code Zero* (2017) and the *Kyd Cadet* trilogy (2010-14). *Grumpy Santa* fit seamlessly into the style he had established, and—for all that he rather self-effacingly admits in the game's instructions that the whole thing took him only a few days to write—the gameplay is accessible, the presentation is refined and the overall playing experience is always appealing.

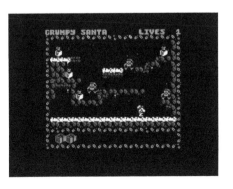

ICICLE WORKS

Statesoft (1985)

It's a strange place, the North Pole. While some people go prospecting for gold, platinum or other rare metals, the protagonist of *Icicle Works* finds himself mining the frozen ground for... toys? Over the course of thirteen different levels, the player must construct various playthings—ranging from model planes to beach balls—from component parts that are scattered around the level. In some cases, the toy fragments are stored within containers which must be smashed open before their contents can be gathered. In later stages, enemies such as penguins and polar bears appear and must be avoided or crushed with falling snowballs. Similarly, if ice cold Arctic water is released then it will rapidly flood the area, making parts of the room inaccessible. Only once the toy has been fully constructed (the completed item appears in a section on the bottom-right of the screen) can the player escape through one of the level's exits and reach the next stage.

Icicle Works is an entertaining riff on the well-known style of First Star/Front Runner's *Boulderdash* (1984), with the game's dynamics—digging through snow rather than earth, and heavy items plunging downward when the snow beneath them is displaced—proving to be largely unchanged from the original game. *Icicle Works* was developed by Richard Parratt, who is perhaps better recognised for his game creation utility *The Dungeon Builder* (1984) for Dream Software which was released the previous year. While graphically *Icicle Works* may not be the most aesthetically attractive title for the Spectrum, with jerky scrolling and unresponsive controls letting the side down at times, the levels are presented with a

decent amount of variety and the challenge of collecting every necessary piece of the missing toy on each level is ameliorated somewhat by the fact that there are sometimes a number of different copies of the same section located nearby. However, the player is usually presented with a quandary; either find a way of gathering a proximate but inconveniently-situated section, or spend valuable seconds scouting other areas for another identical piece which may be more accessible. Further complicating things, there is a pretty strict time limit which offers next to no wriggle room to explore the level; strategies must be formulated quickly as the player goes along.

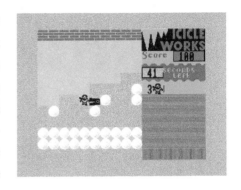

Based in Stevenage, Statesoft was not by any means a prolific software publisher for the Spectrum; beyond *Icicle Works*, the company's only other release for the machine was *Bristles* (1984), a platform action game based around home decorating. *Icicle Works* was widely reviewed at the time of its release, but computer magazine critics gave a very tepid response. While the standard of the graphics and the lack of music met with disapproval, some reviewers praised the cerebral puzzles and the fine balance of action and brainwork required to progress through the game. Generally, however, the feeling was that *Boulderdash* clones had become so plentiful by this stage, any new take on the game's format would need to present something quite fresh and new… and *Icicle Works* didn't offer quite enough originality to really stand out from an increasingly well-populated crowd.

With its abundance of snow and Arctic wildlife, *Icicle Works* certainly contained plenty of wintry atmosphere, while its toy-gathering objective placed it safely within the confines of the Christmas game genre. In the presentation of its action it may not have been the most innovative title, but with its glacial palette and demanding time constraints there was certainly no small amount of playability. Ultimately, however, the likelihood of sticking with the game to the end is likely to depend on whether a player considers its goals to be more rewarding than frustrating.

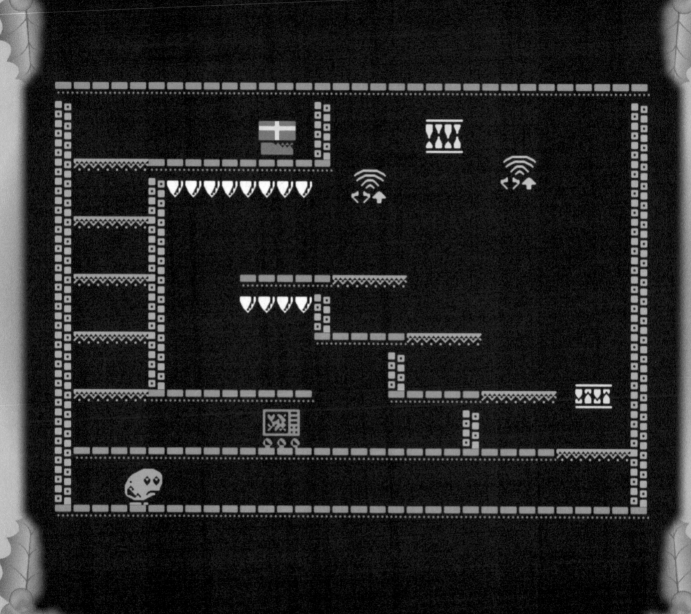

SPROUTY

Stonechat Productions (2019)

Has there ever been a more maligned staple of Christmas than the humble Brussels Sprout? First appearing in the 5th century and eventually being cultivated in the region of Brussels in Belgium (from where their distinctive name originated) in the 13th century, this small leaf vegetable has become popular across Europe and North America as a Christmas dinner supplement... even though their tastiness has been hotly contested over the years, with some people loving them and others detesting them with just as much vigour. But while they may well be the ultimate 'love them or hate them' festive food, one thing is certain—they aren't exactly the most immediate choice as the protagonist of a computer game.

Step forward programmer Dave Hughes, who has laboured to rehabilitate the reputation of the Brussels Sprout and make it the hero it was always meant to be. *Sprouty* follows the travails of the affable tiny cabbage as he makes his way through eighteen playable levels in search of his Christmas presents. You may well think that the festive season would be a tough time for a sprout, facing the prospect of being boiled for consumption along with turkey and bread sauce, but this particular specimen is so excited about Christmas that he is repeatedly jumping for joy. That is to say, the player only controls the character's left and right movements, as whenever he becomes stationery he instinctively jumps up and down on the spot.

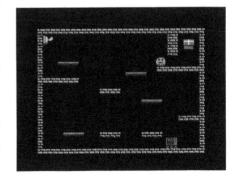

Sprouty's spontaneous jumping adds an additional layer of difficulty to the game, as to hop over obstacles and enemies his movements must be timed precisely so that he will spring up at the right point. Unfortunately

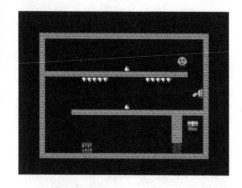

if he should fall from a certain height, he will be momentarily stunned which makes accurate timing more challenging that it might seem at first. Additionally, gates on various screens are operated by flicking switches, so Sprouty will need to ensure that he plans his course around each level in order to reach every parcel safely.

Created with the *Arcade Game Designer*, *Sprouty* is full of presentational elegance—there is impressive musical accompaniment by 'Djnzx48' on the 128K version (as usual, just spot effects for 48k users), the sprites are cute and colourful with smooth motion, and the game was released in numerous different languages to ensure accessibility for players all over the world. While it's true that Sprouty's impromptu jumping takes a bit of getting used to, the game's difficulty level has been carefully deliberated to give everyone plenty of opportunity to acclimatise to the character's impulsive movements before the action becomes more taxing.

As might be expected, the level layouts progressively turn more tricky as the game continues; because Sprouty must complete each screen in turn, there is always a chance to try out different strategies as the player makes their way through the stages. Without imposing a limit on either the player's lives of the amount of time required to finish a level, the game has a nicely relaxed feel which chimes in perfectly with its yuletide setting.

With its whimsical selection of enemies and a faultlessly-pitched level of difficulty, this is the kind of platform action game which requires a bit of thought before jumping right into each level and attempting to collect Sprouty's gift in every stage. Though the thing is, the idea of a smiling, bouncing sprout isn't even the most fanciful aspect of *Sprouty*. Rather, it's the fact that—given most people can barely tolerate Brussels Sprouts and try to hide them in their napkin before the dessert course, much less love them—it's nothing short of a miracle that good old Sprouty was popular enough to have been given eighteen presents in the first place.

SANTA

Top Spec (1987)

Based in East Molesey in Surrey, Top Spec Software was a relatively short-lived developer which arguably became best-known for its sporting-themed titles such as *F.A. Cup* (1986), *Goalie* (1986), *Striker* (1986) and *League Winners* (1986). In 1987, however, they were to make their sole foray into the world of Christmas software in the form of *Santa*.

The game's minimal instructions explain that Santa Claus must collect parcels from five different screens before being tasked with delivering them all without crashing his sleigh. Easier said than done, as poor old Father Christmas was rarely so crudely drawn nor as jerkily controlled than when he appeared here. If the player can vary the height and position of the sleigh to collect the gifts, it's on to the next stage... and more of the same.

Being released at a 'premium budget' price point of £3.99, *Santa* was ignored by trade press reviewers at the time of its release... and with respect to the creators, it's easy to see why, as in terms of graphics and gameplay it would have seemed archaic even by the early-to-mid-eighties. The whole undertaking looks like a type-in program printed in a computer magazine, with erratic movement, simplistic sprites and the inescapable sense that the whole thing had been written in BASIC—in a very short period of time.

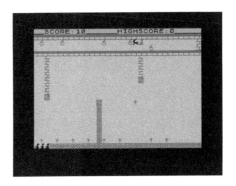

The release did contain a degree of value for money, as the cassette's B-side contained flip-screen platform game *Haunted House* (1986), crossword simulator *Specword* (1986) and vertically-scrolling space action title *Upman* (1986). Unfortunately all of them shared the same elementary graphics and unrefined presentation.

CHRISTMAS CRAPMAS

Andrew Gillen (2017)

Ooh err! Santa's gone bonkers!

You have to admire a game that puts its intent front and centre in the title: *Christmas Crapmas* is an unashamedly retro slice of Spectrum action that very much looks back to the machine's earliest titles for its inspiration. Don't be fooled by its self-effacing name or the unsophisticated graphics, however—beneath the veneer of artlessness lies gameplay that is hard as nails.

The story behind the game is fairly basic: Santa Claus must scour every level collecting parcels from under the noses of 'the guardians'—enemies who prowl around looking to stop Father Christmas in his tracks. Once he has collected a gift, the square it previously occupied will turn into a section of brick wall, meaning that neither Santa nor any of the other characters can pass through it. This may sound like a minor point, but given the narrow areas Santa has to squeeze through (even worse than a household chimney), tackling the presents in the wrong order can see him trapped between a rock and a hard place.

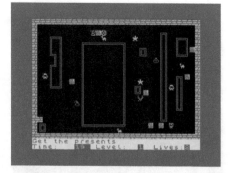

Not that there's much time to plan his course of action, as there's a pretty tight time limit in place which starts ticking down the second the level begins. Nor can Santa rely on the gifts always being in the same place, as there is a degree of randomness in their locations which means that the same strategies won't always work from one playthrough to the next. Once

Santa has started moving, he keeps on going in a straight line until the player diverts his course along another vector. This relies on some pretty fast reactions, as while some of Santa's opponents follow predictable paths he will soon find that others are much more erratic in their movements—and consequently prove to be significantly more difficult to avoid. Each level brings with it a new wave of obstacles to overcome, and with them new tactics to put into play.

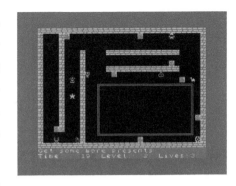

Christmas Crapmas first appeared on *WOOT! Tape Magazine*'s 'ZXmas' 2017 Edition and was the work of Andrew Gillen, whose Christmas credentials had already been cemented thanks to his *Good King Wenceslas Simulator* (2012). Gillen has been responsible for numerous other Spectrum titles, many of them pleasingly tongue-in-cheek in nature, which have included *Snailympics* (2012), *Dave Infuriators* (2012), *Advanced Superior Space Invaders 2600 Conversion Simulator ZX* (2013) and *Spiker: Basic Training* (2013). He has also been active as a programmer for the SAM Coupé, the ambitious but short-lived 8-bit home computer system released by Swansea's Miles Gordon Technology in 1989.

Produced using Dave Hughes's *Classic Game Designer* (2013), a game creation utility with a focus on 'old school' retro titles, it seems fair to say that *Christmas Crapmas* was certainly never going to win any prizes for graphical excellence. As games go, it had no affectations beyond serving up a challenging slice of festive keyboard-hammering that would tax its players' grey matter as well as their manual dexterity.

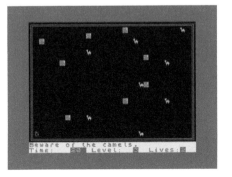

While it may not necessarily look like the most overtly jolly game to accompany your yuletide celebrations, *Christmas Crapmas* offers far more playability than its name suggests—and as losing all three lives will see Santa sent straight back to the very beginning of the game, there is a definite 'just one more go' sense of addictiveness as the player is encouraged to battle onwards to complete the last level.

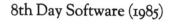

8th Day Software (1985)

In the frozen polar wastes, trouble is afoot... and it has nothing to do with Santa's workshop for once. An international terrorist named Stirling has infiltrated a remote research station and is holding New York City to ransom with an atomic device. In the role of a secret service agent, the player's task is to make their way across the dangerous ice field, overcoming numerous environmental obstacles as they go, in an effort to confront Stirling by stealth and neutralise him before he has a chance to make good on his threats and set off the nuclear weapon.

Ice Station Zero has an interesting history, in that it was first released in 1985 by Wirral's 8th Day Software as part of their *Games Without Frontiers* cycle—a series of budget text adventure titles priced at £1.75 each, which spanned various genres and included games such as *Four Minutes to Midnight* (1985), *Cuddles* (1984), *Quann Tualla* (1985), *In Search of Angels* (1985) and *Faerie* (1985). Many computer magazine reviewers of the time reacted enthusiastically to high-quality interactive fiction being released at such an affordable price, and *Ice Station Zero*—having initially been a text-only game—was reissued in slightly different revisions before eventually being re-released in 1989 with a range of graphical illustrations at £2.99.

Created with *The Quill*, the game does not by any means boast the most expansive parser, but the action is judiciously paced and the puzzles are well-constructed. There is obvious effort in the stark prose to create an atmospheric environment where the harsh elements are working against the player's efforts, and where plausible dangers (and a few outlandish ones) lurk around every corner. There is a fairly sizeable red herring in evidence near the beginning of the game, and not all of the collectable items will necessarily be equally useful once the protagonist's icy trek gets underway. However, the journey is laced with situations that owe much to thriller writers such as Alistair MacLean and Ian Fleming, and anyone looking for some snowy derring-do will find much to enjoy.

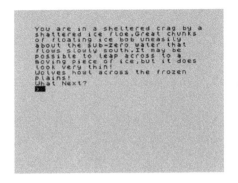

That being said, the game is not without its occasional irritations. Several critics flagged up the issue with the pack of wolves which stalk the player indefatigably throughout the game, and which will pounce at the first sign of weakness. They can be outmanoeuvred (in which case they will almost certainly reappear at the least convenient juncture) or be scared off at the sound of a gun firing. However, the shot has to sound at exactly the right time, or the wolves will be back again undaunted by the player's efforts. Thankfully they soon disperse once the agent reaches a certain glacier.

Especially for a budget title, the game requires a fair bit of effort to complete; certainly anyone shelling out for it would not have been disappointed by the length of the mission that awaited them. While not all of the hazards the player will encounter are necessarily as believable as the central premise—a tribe of cannibals have to be overcome at one point, as does an angry yeti and a surprisingly persistent pterodactyl—once they reach the titular research base the action becomes rather more technologically focused as the agent races to locate Stirling and disarm the missile.

Ice Station Zero was the work of Mike E. Turner, whose other text adventures for the Spectrum had included *A Spell of Christmas Ice* (q.v.), amongst others. On the reverse side of the game cassette, at least with some releases, was *How to Play Adventures* (1985), 8th Day Software's instructional simulator designed for people who were new to interactive fiction and wanted to learn the fundamentals of this category of game prior to tackling the adventure itself.

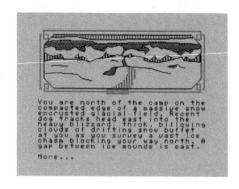

You are north of the camp on the compacted edge of a massive snow encrusted glacial field. Recent dog tracks head east into the heavy blizzard. thick, billowing clouds of drifting snow buffet at you as you survey a vast ice chasm blocking your way north. A gap between ice mounds is east.

More...

Critics were initially unconvinced by the merits of *Ice Station Zero*, and opinion was divided at the time of its release. While many approved of the game's ambition and praised the value for money it presented, others considered it formulaic and occasionally frustrating. Some positivity was expressed for the graphical accompaniment on later editions of the game, which presented suitably austere illustrations to coincide with the freezing subzero surroundings where the action takes place.

While there is no doubting that the game presents an unusual clash of styles in its presentation of stark techno-thriller realism on one hand and eccentric encounters with fantasy creatures on the other, the incongruity never conspires to make the game any less entertaining. The documentation suggests that *Ice Station Zero* is particularly suitable for beginners to text adventure gaming, and while this is reflected in the limitations of the game's vocabulary and the comparatively small number of objects to be found and used, the game itself is certainly no push-over. While the puzzles aren't necessarily the most complex to overcome, they are fairly abundant in number, and the player will certainly want to sketch out a map of the well-thought-out range of locations which make up the frozen wasteland of the game's setting.

You are spinning on a thin isle of moving ice in a semi frozen crack of moving water and ice. A further extension of this block of ice is east of you, but on closer investigation it would appear to be thinner than this one. The near bank is within easy jumping distance westwards.

More...

As was the case with many popular text adventures, *Ice Station Zero* was re-released by G.I. Games in 1991 and, later, by Zenobi Software in 1993. This allowed the game to be enjoyed by entirely new audiences long after its initial release, even once the Spectrum's glory days had passed. It has since gone on to become one of 8th Day Software's best-remembered titles, and set a high watermark for the level of quality that was possible on a budget-priced text adventure. Though admittedly not exactly brimming with festive *joie de vivre*, anyone seeking an enlivening sojourn through icy surroundings in search of espionage action is unlikely to be disappointed by this stimulating and often surprising title.

ZOMBO'S CHRISTMAS CAPERS

Monsterbytes (2016)

From *The Walking Dead* to *World War Z*, there are few aspects of modern pop culture more ubiquitous than zombies. While the presence of reanimated corpses makes perfect sense in a suspense horror narrative, however, they have generally not been all that closely associated with Christmas adventures... until now, that is.

Created by Henry Flint and Al Ewing, the *Zombo* character first appeared in the famous *2000AD* fantasy/sci-fi anthology comic back in 2009. Zombo is a human/zombie hybrid with a surprisingly polite manner who lives in a far-future setting, where he was created as a biological weapon with the ability to survive in environments too hostile for human habitation. To date, Zombo has made two appearances in unofficial games written for the Spectrum: *Zombo* (2015), and then *Zombo's Christmas Capers* a year later.

Like its predecessor, *Zombo's Christmas Capers* is an action adventure. Santa has unexpectedly gone missing from his workshop after an unfortunately-timed nervous breakdown. Zombo has been tasked by the government with tracking down the lost Father Christmas as well as gathering up all of the gifts intended for children on the 'nice list' (which number only six in total, due to most kids being on the 'naughty list' in 2016). In addition to finding Santa and each of the presents, Zombo must also find a way of defeating

Zombo is Copyright © Henry Flint/Al Ewing/Rebellion Developments

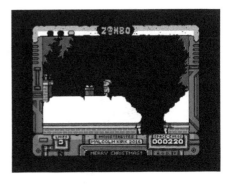

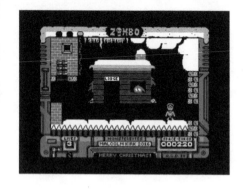

the fearsome end-of-game boss. To this end, a variety of items can be found on his travels which include colour-coded keys and the handy Shootybang 2000 gun (which, as the instructions reveal, has the unfortunate restriction of only being able to fire horizontally).

The game was created by Malcolm Kirk, whose other games for the Spectrum have included the similarly zombie-themed *Dead by Dawn* (2012), impressive 3D werewolf adventure *Loups Garoux* (1993) and the 2000AD-inspired *Dredd Over Eels* (2017)—in which lethal lawman Judge Dredd finds himself the surprising star of a Jon Ritman/Bernie Drummond-style isometric adventure. *Zombo's Christmas Capers* was programmed using the *Arcade Game Designer*, and really makes the most of the halcyon game creation utility to create a highly distinctive and, at times, rather surreal playing environment.

With 27 playable screens to explore, Zombo (whose sprite seems unusually cute for a mobile decaying cadaver) has a fair bit of ground to cover. The game is full of inspired pop cultural references, from an intriguing appearance of the enigmatic Black Lodge/'Red Room' from *Twin Peaks* through to a copy of the 2000AD annual turning up rather randomly as a collectable item. In a rather nice touch, players are constantly reminded of Zombo's hybrid status as he can be seen breathing throughout the game—which would otherwise be quite a nifty trick for someone who is a corpse!

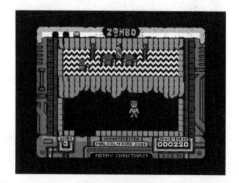

While some enemies follow predictable paths, others can be a bit more difficult to avoid so a smidgen of lateral thinking may be required. With its colourful graphics and absurd situations, the game is fun to delve into, and Zombo makes for an amiable companion. Though the experience sadly lacks any musical accompaniment, there is a very inventive custom loader that is bound to encourage a grin. As for the plot... whatever did happen to the missing Santa? Well, you'll just have to play through the game if you want to find out!

CHRIMBLAST

Stonechat Productions (2015)

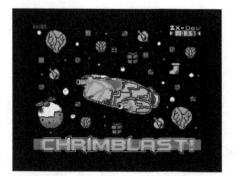

If the Spectrum ever needed a Christmas version of a vertically-scrolling shoot-'em-up in the style of *Galaga*, programmer Dave Hughes took up the reins to ensure that its users were not disappointed—and in high style, as it happens, for the result provided plenty of explosive bang for their buck.

Chrimblast is a no-holds-barred explosion-fest which throws players straight into the centre of the action. Once the joystick of choice has been selected (or the keyboard controls have been defined), it's right into the thick of things as the player's craft starts scrolling up into the endless void of space. Waiting for them are wave after wave of enemies, some of which have a Christmas theme while others have more overtly sci-fi origins.

The game's objective is to keep the bad guys at bay while collecting festive items such as wrapped presents, roast turkeys and so forth. Naturally, however, the enemies react in different ways, with some proving unusually difficult to shake while others require several direct hits before they are destroyed. Gameplay becomes more tricky the further the player advances, but it's worth persevering if only to see what surprises Christmas game supremo Hughes is keeping up his sleeve.

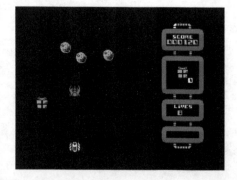

The 128K version of the game features some excellent music from Poland's 'Yerzmyey', while there is also a fair bit of digitised speech in evidence which adds an extra touch of class to proceedings. While it's certainly not the most sophisticated gameplay you'll ever see in a Spectrum Christmas game, the presentation is slick, and for a blast through an endless succession of bad guys it's a pleasing distraction.

FRANTIC PENGO

Gabriele Amore (2021)

It says everything for the versatility of the Sinclair ZX Spectrum that developers are still producing brand new games for that venerable early eighties hardware even now, in the present day. At time of writing, the most recent seasonal title to appear for the system is Gabriele Amore's *Frantic Pengo*, which first appeared in January 2021.

A sequel of sorts to Amore's earlier game *Pengo Quest* (2015), *Frantic Pengo* sees the eponymous penguin on a quest to rescue his girlfriend Penga who has been kidnapped by lava monsters. Reasoning that creatures with a high body temperature might just be susceptible to being crushed by blocks of ice, Pengo sets off to clear level after level of bad guys in order to clear a path to Penga. The ice blocks can be shoved horizontally or vertically to collide with the lava monsters, but Pengo also has the ability to destroy blocks if he necessary—and can even create a handy shortcut from one side of the screen to the other by breaking through the ice barrier forming a border around the playing area.

With a total of 14 playable screens, Pengo has only three lives to get the job done, while a restrictive time limit on every level means that the player doesn't have a lot of wiggle room to clear their opponents out. There is some inspired level design in evidence, however, so every stage poses different challenges and will require particular strategies to be employed if Pengo is to emerge triumphant (and in one piece).

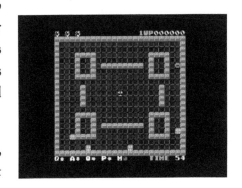

Gabriele Amore has been a very prolific programmer on the Spectrum, having produced games including *Push 'n' Chase* (2013), *Leonardo's Lost Last*

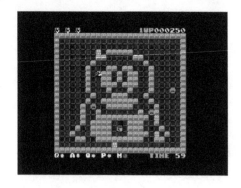

Invention (2014), *Baffo Jones* (2015), *Bubble Frenzy* (2016) and *Jungle Queen* (2020), amongst dozens of others. Having covered many different genres, *Frantic Pengo* fits nicely into their *oeuvre*; the style of its arcade action owes a great deal to Coreland/Sega's *Pengo* (1982), but always with enough thoughtful innovation to keep the action fresh.

Created in *AGDx Mini*, a modification of the *Arcade Game Designer*, *Frantic Pengo* is a 128K only game with music provided by Pedro Pimenta. The title track has a very retro eighties feel, being a more than competent cover version of Ryan Paris's synthesiser classic *Dolce Vita* (1983), but the rhythm of the original in-game tune has every bit as much potential for foot-tapping.

The keyboard controls are intuitive, and are displayed at the base of the screen throughout the action—which makes it doubly unlikely that players will be inclined to forget any of them mid-game. *Frantic Pengo* provides plenty of enjoyment for its players, but in spite of the familiarity of the gameplay it is no pushover to complete; between the time constraints and the adroit artificial intelligence of the enemies, whose movements are far from predictable, Pengo will need to be fast on his flippers if he intends to outmanoeuvre and trap all of the monsters on each level.

Frantic Pengo may be the most recent seasonal game to be released for the Spectrum, but thanks to the machine's hard-working homebrew scene it is unlikely to be the last. Perhaps the greatest compliment that can be paid to festive software on the Spectrum is that even now, almost forty years after Sinclair Research released the system to the public, there is still no such thing as an archetypal Christmas game on the platform—such is the inventiveness of programmers over the years, the games which have appeared have continued to entertain and puzzle in equal measure... and with interest in this most quintessentially 1980s of microcomputers still showing no sign of diminishing all these decades later, surely many more yuletide titles are still to come.

ABOUT THE AUTHOR

Dr Thomas Christie has many years of experience as a literary and publishing professional, working in collaboration with several companies including Cambridge Scholars Publishing, Crescent Moon Publishing, Robert Greene Publishing and Applause Books. A passionate advocate of the written word and literary arts, over the years he has worked to develop original writing for respected organisations such as the Stirling Smith Art Gallery and Museum and a leading independent higher education research unit based at the University of Stirling. His work has featured at international venues including Paris and Rio de Janeiro. Additionally, he is regularly involved in public speaking events and has delivered guest lectures and presentations about his work at many locations around the United Kingdom. He is co-director of Extremis Publishing.

Tom was elected a Fellow of the Royal Society of Arts in 2018, and is a member of the Royal Society of Literature, the Society of Authors, the Federation of Writers Scotland and the Authors' Licensing and Collecting Society. He holds a first-class Honours degree in English Literature and a Master's degree in Humanities with British Cinema History from the Open University in Milton Keynes, and a Doctorate in Scottish Literature awarded by the University of Stirling.

He is the author of a number of books on the subject of modern film which include *Liv Tyler: Star in Ascendance* (2007), *The Cinema of Richard Linklater* (2008), *John Hughes and Eighties Cinema: Teenage Hopes and American Dreams* (2009), *Ferris Bueller's Day Off: Pocket Movie Guide* (2010), *The Christmas Movie Book* (2011), *The James Bond Movies of the 1980s* (2013), *Mel Brooks: Genius and Loving It!: Freedom and Liberation in the Cinema of Mel Brooks* (2015), *A Righteously Awesome Eighties Christmas: Festive Cinema of the 1980s* (2016), *John Hughes FAQ* (2019) and *The Golden Age of Christmas Movies: Festive Cinema of the 1940s and 50s* (2019).

His other works include *Notional Identities: Ideology, Genre and National Identity in Popular Scottish Fiction Since the Seventies* (2013), *The Spectrum of Adventure: A Brief History of Interactive Fiction on the Sinclair ZX Spectrum* (2016), *Contested Mindscapes: Exploring Approaches to Dementia in Modern Popular Culture* (2018), and – in collaboration with his sister, Julie Christie – *The Heart 200 Book: A Companion Guide to Scotland's Most Exciting Road Trip* (2020). He has also written a crowdfunded murder-mystery novel, *The Shadow in the Gallery* (2013), which is set during the nineteenth century in Stirling's historic Smith Art Gallery and Museum.

For more details about Tom and his work, please visit his website at: www.tomchristiebooks.co.uk

Also Available from Extremis Publishing

THE SPECTRUM OF ADVENTURE
By Thomas A. Christie

The Sinclair ZX Spectrum was one of the most popular home computers in British history, selling over five million units in its 1980s heyday. Amongst the thousands of titles released for the Spectrum during its lifetime, the text adventure game was to emerge as one of the most significant genres on the system.

Covering 100 games in all, this book celebrates the Spectrum's thriving interactive fiction scene of the eighties, chronicling the achievements of major publishers as well as independent developers from the machine's launch in 1982 until the end of the decade in 1989.

Examining titles by some of the best-known software houses of the eighties – including Magnetic Scrolls, Level 9 Computing, Delta 4 Software, St Bride's School and many others – *The Spectrum of Adventure* explores what it was about this distinctive period in computing history that produced so many compelling interactive fiction games.

So make sure that you fill your lamp with oil, dust down your verb-noun interface, and get ready for a nostalgic trip through colossal caves, deserted spacecraft, political satire, genre parodies and much more besides.

A RIGHTEOUSLY AWESOME EIGHTIES CHRISTMAS
By Thomas A. Christie

The cinema of the festive season has blazed a trail through the world of film-making for more than a century, ranging from silent movies to the latest CGI features. From the author of *The Christmas Movie Book*, this new text explores the different narrative themes which emerged in the genre over the course of the 1980s, considering the developments which have helped to make the Christmas films of that decade amongst the most fascinating and engaging motion pictures in the history of festive movie production.

Released against the backdrop of a turbulent and rapidly-changing world, the Christmas films of the 1980s celebrated traditions and challenged assumptions in equal measure. With warm nostalgia colliding with aggressive modernity as never before, the eighties saw the movies of the holiday season being deconstructed and reconfigured to remain relevant in an age of cynicism and innovation.

Whether exploring comedy, drama, horror or fantasy, Christmas cinema has an unparalleled capacity to attract and inspire audiences. With a discussion ranging from the best-known titles to some of the most obscure, *A Righteously Awesome Eighties Christmas* examines the ways in which the Christmas motion pictures of the 1980s fit into the wider context of this captivating and ever-evolving genre.

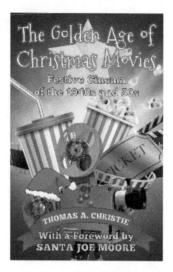

THE GOLDEN AGE OF CHRISTMAS MOVIES
By Thomas A. Christie

Today the Christmas movie is considered one of the best-loved genres in modern cinema, entertaining audiences across the globe with depictions of festive celebrations, personal reinvention and the enduring value of friendship and family. But how did the themes and conventions of this category of film come to take form, and why have they proven to be so durable that they continue to persist and be reinvented even in the present day?

From the author of *A Righteously Awesome Eighties Christmas*, this book takes a nostalgic look back at the Christmas cinema of the 1940s and 50s, including a discussion of classic films which came to define the genre. Considering the unforgettable storylines and distinctive characters that brought these early festive movies to life, it discusses the conventions which were established and the qualities which would define Christmas titles for decades to come.

Examining landmark features such as *It's a Wonderful Life*, *Miracle on 34th Street*, *The Bishop's Wife* and *White Christmas*, *The Golden Age of Christmas Movies* delves into some of the most successful festive films ever produced, and also reflects upon other movies of the time that—for one reason or another—have all but disappeared into the mists of cinema history. Considering films which range from the life-affirming to the warmly sentimental, *The Golden Age of Christmas Movies* investigates the many reasons why these memorable motion pictures have continued to entertain generations of moviegoers.

For details of new and forthcoming books from Extremis Publishing, including our monthly podcasts, please visit our official website at:

www.extremispublishing.com

or follow us on social media at:

www.facebook.com/extremispublishing

www.linkedin.com/company/extremis-publishing-ltd-/

CPSIA information can be obtained
at www.ICGtesting.com
Printed in the USA
LVHW061618140921
697808LV00006B/189

9 781999 696290